A Study in Regional Taste
The May Show 1919-1975

Published by The Cleveland Museum of Art

A Study in Regional Taste
The May Show 1919-1975

Jay Hoffman
Dee Driscole
Mary Clare Zahler

Photographic Credits

Jay Hoffman, author of the essay *The May Show: History and Heritage,* is an instructor in the Department of Art History and Education at The Cleveland Museum of Art. Dee Driscole and Mary Clare Zahler are both students in the Department of Art at Cleveland State University; they are the authors of the numerous artists' biographies included. The exhibition was organized under the guidance of Gabriel P. Weisberg and Andrew T. Chakalis of the Department of Art History and Education of The Cleveland Museum of Art.

Martin Linsey, Staff Photographer,
  Department of Art History and Education
The Cleveland Museum of Art Photography Studio

Frontispiece:
Gallery X. First annual exhibition by Cleveland
artists and craftsmen, May 2-June 29, 1919.
Photo: The Cleveland Museum of Art.

Copyright 1977 by The Cleveland Museum of Art

Hoffman, Jay.
  A study in regional taste.
Catalog of an exhibition, held July 13-Aug. 1, 1977,
giving a retrospective view of The Cleveland Museum of
Art's May Show, 1919-1975.
  1. Art, American—Ohio—Exhibitions. 2. Art,
Modern—20th century—Ohio—Exhibitions. I. Driscole,
Dee, joint author. II. Zahler, Mary Clare, joint
author. III. Cleveland Museum of Art. IV. Title.
N6530.03H63   759.13'074'0177132   77-78145
ISBN 0-910386-36-6

The catalogue has been made possible through a special grant provided by the John P. Murphy Foundation

Preface

The evolution of the May Show, from a small regional exhibition to one eagerly anticipated by artists and collectors of the northeastern Ohio area, has interested local historians not only for the contribution the show has made to regional art but also for the role played by the Museum in responding to the interests of a community and in supporting local artists. From its inception the May Show was endorsed by the directors of The Cleveland Museum of Art—especially William M. Milliken (director from 1930 to 1958), who recognized that this was one way art could be encouraged during the difficult Depression years. Since 1958 Sherman E. Lee has maintained a vigorous support of the May Shows, modifying some aspects, but reinforcing the commitment of the Museum to its local constituents.

In preparing a brief history of the May Show and in attempting to locate examples of quality that were previously exhibited, art historians and curators were assisted by artists' relatives, friends, and collectors. An effort was made to obtain a broad sample of objects so that a fair survey could be reassembled. This task took considerable time and effort; but the rewards were many, as long-forgotten works brought out of storage and others were reassessed by a new May Show jury eager to see how the objects had weathered the test of time. The final flowering is the retrospective itself which draws from past exhibitions but with a new approach—exhibiting objects of quality which were previously shown, while at the same time recreating the atmosphere and heritage which made the May Show such a vital phenomenon in the cultural life of Cleveland.

No exhibition of this type would be complete without first locating the published materials that provide the documentary sources for further investigation of the past. The CMA *Bulletin,* the Registrar's archives, as well as discussions with appropriate curators such as Edward B. Henning and Tom Hinson—both intimately connected with the tradition of the May Show—provided valuable insights into the ways in which such an exhibition could be focused. The writings of local art historians, especially Dr. Karal Ann Marling, formerly on the staff of Case Western Reserve University, maintained our enthusiasm as we examined published materials on the Federal Arts Program and the support of local artists by William M. Milliken. Her essay on "William M. Milliken and Federal Art Patronage of the Depression Decade" (CMA *Bulletin,* December 1974) and her catalog dedicated to *Federal Art in Cleveland: 1933-1943* (Cleveland, 1974) provided valuable assistance in giving us a clearer picture of the art activity against which the May Show must be seen. With this matrix understood, it was possible to obtain the assistance of art history students who with Jay Hoffman, instructor in the Department of Art History and Education, began the process of interviewing local artists and selecting objects for the exhibition. Without the enthusiasm of Dee Driscole and Mary Clare Zahler, art history students at Cleveland State University, much of the field work necessary for a show as complex as this one could not have been accomplished in such a short time. The fruit of their research is found in the excellent biographical statements on nine of the key artists who continuously contributed to past May Shows.

Enthusiastic support for the concept of the show came from local collectors and relatives of artists who had contributed to past shows. The family of Frederick Biehle assisted in locating early works by August Biehle, thereby completing a picture of the type of paintings found in the May Shows of the 1920's; Joseph Erdelac opened his extensive archives and collection and continually encouraged us to locate the best examples of region-

Contents

al artists; and Bernice Kent assisted in securing examples of the crafts tradition which have always been found in the May Shows. Other collectors, too numerous to mention, came to our assistance following our call for objects. Their kindness and generosity is acknowledged even if space did not permit our using the objects they suggested. An exhibition of about ninety pieces cannot do justice to the broad spectrum of examples available in the Cleveland area.

Special recognition should be given Andrew T. Chakalis, supervisor of the Extensions Division, who diligently assisted in securing local objects and recognized the pitfalls that had to be overcome if the show were going to succeed. His intuitive grasp of the local heritage helped us draw together the diverse strains of this exhibition. Janet Leonard, secretary to the curator of Art History and Education, typed the manuscript with precision and expertise. The support of Merald E. Wrolstad, Sally W. Goodfellow, and Martin Linsey must also be acknowledged in the editing, production of the catalog, and photographic work. The photo studio, and especially Nicholas C. Hlobeczy, assisted us in innumerable ways as we endeavored to secure good photographs for this catalog.

Gabriel P. Weisberg, Curator
Department of Art History & Education

Introduction

One of the first annual regional exhibitions in the country, the Cleveland May Show has continued for fifty-nine years with but one interruption (when the Education Wing of the Museum was being built in 1970). During this period of time its character has undergone many changes, reflecting both international tendencies in the arts and local predilections. From its beginning in 1919 through 1957, the May Show emerged as one of the largest and most successful of all regional shows. Under William M. Milliken's able guidance, it established a tradition of sales records which continues to the present and is unequaled by any other regional exhibition. During the 1930's in particular, many artists would have been forced to abandon their chosen field had it not been for sales made from the May Show. The emphasis on sales not only benefited artists materially but also psychologically. During a period when the arts were either abandoned or supported by public funds, those selling works from the May Show took pride in the fact that they were at least partially self-supporting.

Besides encouraging creative artists, the May Show has also benefited collectors. A purchase from the May Show has often been the first step for someone who has continued to collect art while coming to recognize the emotional and intellectual stimulation of life in the company of works of art.

Changes which have occurred over the years in the mechanics of the exhibition have been largely dictated by changed economic conditions and efforts to respond to the needs of the growing professional art community in Northeastern Ohio. Certain other modifications reflect events that have occurred in the art community itself. For example, the merging of many categories into four general classifications—Painting, Sculpture, Graphics, and Crafts—indicates the breakdown of rigorous, traditional concepts of style, technique, material, and subject matter. Indeed, many works submitted to the May Show still straddle two or more of the remaining four broad categories.

It is difficult, if not impossible, to clearly define all the ingredients necessary for an artistically active and successful community. Yet some features seem to be essential: for example, (1) an open society which allows talent to assert itself; (2) the means to train and educate those who are so gifted; (3) opportunities for artists to exchange ideas with colleagues from other artistically active communities; (4) the chance to experience actual works of art from other cultures; (5) occasions to exhibit one's work where it can be seen, criticized, and supported by the community.

The Cleveland Museum of Art provides opportunities for artists, and the public, to develop their knowledge and taste by viewing and studying major works of art from other times and places. But most importantly, with the May Show it provides a forum where local artists can exhibit their work—to be seen, discussed, measured against their colleagues' work, and acquired by the art public.

The Cleveland Museum has performed these functions for fifty-nine years and it has every intention of continuing to do so.

Sherman E. Lee, Director

List of Lenders

Mr. and Mrs. Jon Alder
Mr. and Mrs. Frederick A. Biehle
Mr. and Mrs. Donald S. Boucela
The Cleveland Museum of Art,
    Decorative Arts Department
The Cleveland Museum of Art,
    Extensions Division of the
    Department of Art History and Education
The Cleveland Museum of Art,
    Modern Art Department
The Cleveland Museum of Art,
    Prints and Drawings Department
The Cleveland Museum of Art,
    Textiles Department
Mr. and Mrs. Joseph Erdelac
Mrs. Bernice Kent
Mr. and Mrs. Henry Steinberg
The Union Commerce Bank
Mr. and Mrs. Lewis C. Williams

Bibliography

Publications

Wittke, Carl. *The First Fifty Years.* The Cleveland Museum of Art, 1966.
Marling, Karal Ann. "William M. Milliken and Federal Art Patronage of the Depression Decade." *CMA Bulletin,* LXI (December 1974), 360-70.
——————. *Federal Art in Cleveland: 1933-1943.* Cleveland: Cleveland Public Library, 1974.

Archival Sources

Volumes VI through LXII (1919-1975). Artists' files and May Show folders in The Cleveland Museum of Art Library. Conversations and Correspondence with: Sandra August, H. C. Cassill, and Joseph McCullough of The Cleveland Institute of Art; Edward Henning, Martin Linsey, and Ann Lurie of The Cleveland Museum of Art.

The May Show: History and Heritage

Already a major manufacturing center at the turn of the twentieth century, Cleveland was famous throughout the nation and the world as a prime example of the American dream in action. The city's affluence was readily visible in its fine parks and broad avenues lined with stately mansions. While offering a lively and rewarding ambiance for its citizens, Cleveland nevertheless was something of a cultural backwater. True, Western Reserve University was on hand to foster the intellect, and any number of schools, clubs, and societies served the interests of the arts and sciences, but the need for major institutions that would bring the city into the cultural mainstream had yet to be met. The situation was only temporary, for throughout the community people were banding together—offering their skills, enthusiasm, and money—in a common effort to bring the needed institutions into being.

In time, the city boasted a panoply of playhouses, orchestras, museums, and societies that stimulated a dialogue with international culture and enhanced the city's creative potential. One of these was the Cleveland Art Association, whose members were committed to helping local artists. The Association maintained a gallery on their behalf and set an example by purchasing works from artists who otherwise had few outlets in the city for their wares. The Association's ambitions far exceeded its resources however, and in 1915—with the intention of providing artists with a broader base of support—members of the Association approached Frederick Whiting, the newly appointed director of The Cleveland Museum of Art, with a proposal for a yearly art exhibit, to be held at the Museum, that would display the city's talents. A central feature of the proposal was that the exhibit be as broadly based as possible, calling upon the entire spectrum of the fine and applied arts. The Association's sugges-

tions were well received, and preparations to make the exhibit a reality were undertaken. In 1919, after a delay of four years, the Cleveland Exposition of Artists and Craftsmen was opened to the public. From the beginning the constant encouragement of William M. Milliken (first May Show supervisor) supported local artists to exhibit their recent work on a yearly basis.

The First Exhibition

Visitors to the exhibit were greeted with a selection of more than 500 objects submitted by local individuals and businesses. Included were ethnic arts and work by the handicapped. Compared to later exhibits, the 1919 Exposition may have lacked something in finesse. The founding committee allowed each exhibitor to install his own objects and to do so in a location of his own choosing. The unseemly scramble that followed was such that this offer was never repeated. But such problems had little effect upon the general enthusiasm with which the Exposition was received.

The 1919 Exposition firmly established what was to become the standard pattern for later May Shows. All work had to be original, of recent completion, and the exhibitor's own. All entries were juried, and citations were presented to the most accomplished artists from a broad list of categories. Sales of objects were emphasized to encourage both collectors and artists. The provenance of entries was limited to the Cleveland area. And certainly what was to become the dearest tradition of all: the Exposition was to be held in the month of May.

The May Show Emerges

Over the ensuing years the exhibitions have become in the public mind "The May Show." Everyone is still invited to submit, but local business for the most part has given up exhibiting. The show has expanded its scope and now serves a thirteen-county area. The various categories designated for the objects —which at times achieved an extreme state of proliferation —have been honed down. Furthermore, prospective exhibitors no longer have to wait out the weeks of suspense until the postman arrives with news of the jury's decision on the day of the preview, and juries are no longer required to send letters critiquing the entries.

The character of the May Show is derived from four sources: the museum, the artists and craftsmen themselves, the jury, and the public. Of these, the public represents the largest group and is the most difficult to define. All types of people come to see the exhibition. Numbering in the tens of thousands, they are but a segment of a much larger population that takes note.

Two groups are afforded special treatment during the festivities that open a May Show. One represents purchasing power, those who in the previous year bought an object from the show. For a long time there was a club composed of such people. It was called the "Pick-Quick Club" and its members enjoyed the privilege of entering the galleries before the official opening to place an option to buy on one or more objects of their choice. Competition among club members opened purses a little wider— much to the benefit of the artists. The "Pick-Quick Club" is no longer in existence but its function is preserved by a patrons' preview.

The second group represents the power of the word. Reporters and columnists invited to the Museum have an opportunity to discuss the show with members of the staff and later in the galleries to formulate their own thoughts. These people—in their access to the media—constitute the primary link between the show and a public whose opinions will be colored by their statements. But people, nevertheless, make what they will of the May Show and are outspoken in their reactions. During May the usual reticence with which people approach art is set aside and every sort of opinion toward the show and its contents is aired.

The Museum's Role

The Museum plays a pivotal role in keeping the May Show alive. No other institution in the city possesses the various resources— the space, skills, personnel, perhaps even the willpower—to mount such an enterprise. Moreover, the Museum is alone in its willingness to absorb the deficits that each Show incurs.

While most exhibitions at the Museum are scholarly and focused, the May Show is a veritable potpourri—not only in its content but also in its production. It is, in essence, a year-round project. Only a few months separate the tying-up of loose ends from one show and the initial preparations for the next. A good part of the Museum staff participates in the preparations. Most directly involved is the coordinator—a member of the staff— whose responsibility it is to make sure that everything goes smoothly. The first step involves lining up temporary help—tactful and patient people who will man the telephones and keep stacks of paper work under control. Most of them are on hand from beginning to end of the exhibition. Then, one-by-one, the various departments of the Museum are called upon to make their contributions. The designer draws up the posters and later plans the layout of the show itself. The photography studio photographs all the entries receiving prizes or jury mention. The print shop gears up to produce a range of goods from application forms to the labels on the walls; the registrar's office charts the disposition of every entry; the carpenters, painters, gardeners, and utility men prepare the gallery setting and move the works of art; the public relations department issues press releases and stands ready to aid the media in every way. The publications department and a local printer produce the catalog. The education department sets to work preparing lecture series; giving tours of the show; and preparing didactic shows, audio-visual tapes, and publications. Before the show ends, almost every-

Gallery view, May Show, 1926. Photo: The Cleveland Museum of Art.

Seniors of the May Show:
Paul B. Travis, August F. Biehle,
George G. Adomeit, and Frank N. Wilcox, 1955.
Photo: Ray Sommer.

body at the Museum has become involved in one way or another.

With but one exception—when it was moved to the Cleveland Institute of Art during construction of the 1958 addition to the Museum—every May Show has been held in the Museum. (During the 1970 construction the exhibition was cancelled.) The look of the show changed gradually during the 1950s and '60s. The earlier '50s had seen the tentative emergence of a unified exhibition concept in which the old practice of massing works together was abandoned in favor of juxtaposing objects according to their visual affinities. The original exhibition galleries with their long sight-lines and generalized lights began to be modelled and folded with the addition of carpentered walls set at raking angles to the axis of the gallery space. The result was that in the first show held in the new wing in 1958, art was played off against a dramatically articulated and spotlighted space full of changing vistas.

Again, in 1971, with the opening of the Education Wing and its special exhibition areas, opportunities were further offered to present the show to its best advantage. The special exhibition areas were large and uncluttered, with high ceilings and tracks from which could be hung hundreds of lights required to illuminate the space. The ceilings also contained provisions for hanging panels that could be used to subdivide areas into a multiplicity of bays and alcoves. Now, more than ever before, each work of art existed in a space attuned to its own special requirements.

The Jury's Role

The ultimate responsibility for what is and is not exhibited in The May Show rests upon the shoulders of a jury. Each juror (now chosen from the Museum staff) brings to the job an expertise. A staff person from the Prints and Drawings Department, for example, usually contributes to the judging of graphics, and a representative from the post-Renaissance Decorative Arts Department is on hand for the judging of crafts. Those of the staff wishing to submit as artists are excluded from the judging. The jury as a whole represents a wide range of tastes and viewpoints, and it is understood that each juror will consider the objects strictly in terms of their clarity, integrity, and thoughtfulness.

But why the Museum staff? Can't juries be called from the community or brought in from out of town? As a matter of fact, until 1971, every May Show jury was composed of non-residents—strangers to the local scene—who presumably would be free of bias and favoritism. The jury was usually selected to strike a balance among art historians, critics, artists, and directors and curators of other institutions. The neutrality of the jurors was often matched by their eminence, and, over the years, many notables served. There were George Bellows, Edward Steichen, Georgia O'Keeffe, Mrs. Juliana Force, Andrew Ritchie, Yasuo Kuniyoshi, Sam Hunter, Robert Rosenblum, Fairfield Porter, Evan Turner, and Minor White—to choose a few familiar names.

On the whole, the jurors appreciated the purposes of the May Show and acted accordingly. However, in the '60s, new forces at work in the art world (as well as in Cleveland) intruded and led ultimately to the end of invited juries. The jurors who served in 1963 were aware that the show was moving away from its old image as a Midwest regional show emphasizing the sale of multiples. This character was developed during the days when the show was a lifeline for artists who might not otherwise have survived the Depression years. All over the country, jurors were stressing international standards of aesthetic quality. The result in Cleveland was the selection of a handful of accepted objects, and it was only because of arguments advanced by the Director that the show regained some semblance of its usual self.

Public reaction was predictable and strong. Artists—especially those rejected—voiced their dismay at what they felt was the imposition of inappropriate standards, and the Museum staff found itself in the uncomfortable position of accounting for the decisions of a jury that had long since gone home. Again, in 1969, a situation arose in which three jurors reacting adversely to each other's philosophical positions put together a show that drew angry reactions from those who felt that the spirit of the May Show was being violated. It was finally decided that if the staff was to be answerable for jury decisions, it should enjoy the privilege of making those decisions initially. While, as always, each subsequent show has produced its share of disagreements, for the most part, the present policy of employing a Museum jury has been found to work well and the show has flourished.

The Artists and Craftsmen

All of the activities surrounding the May Show are, of course, predicated upon the artists and the craftsmen themselves. They are many, and the thousands of entries submitted yearly are a testimony to the force of their presence in the area.

It is difficult to profile the "average" May Show contributor. It can be said, however, that he or she is likely to be either a student or a teacher or one free to pursue the arts and crafts as an avocation. Judging from the 1975 May Show, the area artist is first a painter and next—in order of diminishing numbers—a photographer, a graphics artist, and a sculptor. The area craftsman works predominantly in ceramics, followed in order by textiles, enamel, or glass, jewelry, or metalwork.

The proportional representation of any kind of art or craft in the show depends upon many variables. Few photographers, for example, exhibited in the early shows; now, however, they play an important role. Their present success is the result of the development of new and more available techniques and equipment, a growing acceptance of these once primarily commercial media as fine art, and a serious effort on the part of the Museum to acquire and exhibit photographs.

Yet, even with the burgeoning popularity of certain new media, none has arisen to seriously threaten the popular prestige of painting which still seems to most express the stylistic and theoretical changes occurring within the art community.

The May Show: Its Composition and Changing Tastes

Paintings

The Cleveland Exposition of Artists and Craftsmen opened six years after the 1913 Armory Show in New York. By this time, the revolutionary implications of European paintings and sculpture shown there had been largely absorbed. Artists such as John Marin, Joseph Stella, and Max Weber were proving that Cubism could be applied in a fresh and revealing manner to the staccato rhythms of American life. But in the first decade of the May Show, very little of the modernist influences—of Cubism, Expressionism, or Dadaism—emerged. Instead, one would have encountered, for the most part, more traditional works, rooted in nineteenth-century concepts of subject and form interpreted through the Munich and Ashcan Schools. The effects of Impressionism and Japanese art were evident in bright tonalities and raking perspectives, but rarely were these kinds of art offered the ultimate flattery of emulation. It was not until the late twenties that a form of geometrically abstract art (aside from textile designs and the like) appeared: this was Art Deco, and its primary form of expression was seen in enameled steel and wrought metal.

Several reasons account for this rejection of modernism. Perhaps the practical tone of mind that existed in Cleveland resisted the formal anarchy that seemed to prevail in modernist art. Local art schools were interested in teaching traditional techniques and skills in representing nature as it actually appeared. Only later did local art students become seriously interested in modernist art.

Although painting in the years prior to World War II followed a basically conservative line, it was nevertheless varied and tended, on the whole, to give a good account of its authors. While a visitor to the May Show was not likely to be startled, neither was he likely to be offended by slipshod standards. Many painters actively submitted paintings over a thirty-year span and were

Gallery view, May Show, 1945. Photo: The Cleveland Museum of Art.

later found to be still enthusiastic about the May Show's overall concept.

As events surrounding the First World War shaped a pervasive sense of Americanism in its painting, so World War II—with the vast movements of people and ideas it set into motion—threw open the doors to a new era of internationalism. Veterans of the war, helped by the G. I. bill, trooped off by the thousands as students to New York and to the capitals of Europe and the Orient. More importantly, they absorbed the intellectual and artistic atmosphere they encountered. Encouraged by their experiences, many artists returned home filled with an enthusiasm for various kinds of Abstraction.

By the early 1950's, Abstract Expressionist paintings were beginning to appear in the May Show—tentatively—as had the Cubist-oriented abstractions of the 1930's. Abstract images entered the May Show through the back door. No category was set aside for them; they were forced to masquerade as representational art. In 1957 Joseph McCullough and Anthony Vaiksnoras, submitting frankly abstract paintings, won awards in the industrial and the landscape categories. In 1961 all painting was included under a blanket designation, but by then Abstract Expressionism had passed its peak and was beginning to slide—never to experience full flowering in Cleveland as it had in New York.

New developments were to influence the May Shows of the 1960's: magazines as agents for the propagation of news and opinion were carrying the burning issues of the moment to every corner of the nation and abroad. Now more than ever it was possible to make a reputation as an artist on the strength of reviews—a point that did not pass unnoticed. In part, under the spell of this magazine phenomenon, art began to abandon its walls, to climb down from its pedestals, to leave the safety of the studio and the gallery, and to take its place in the world. It is at this time that painting—among many other media—began to lose its traditional definition. Canvases came to be the products of their stretchers, to be "things" on the way to uniting with sculpture. In other words, these were difficult times for those who held to older, cherished concepts of art.

The May Show, with its traditional categories, managed to allow for these new developments. The category of "oil painting," for example, was first altered to include the less definite "oil, and related media," and later was simply part of the single category "Painting" which included anything done with colored pigments on a surface. In the 1970's the excitement died down. Issue-oriented art began to make way for a more personal approach. The photograph became an important instrument in the conception of new kinds of illusionism. Painters were more inclined to refine their techniques and styles. Now the variety of paintings in the May Show is greater than ever.

Sculpture

As with painting, the history of sculpture in the May Show can be divided into two periods: pre- and post-World War II. From 1919 until the late 1940s sculpture tended to be equated with pedestal statuary. Each year found one or more centerpiece figures rendered in marble or bronze, usually augmented by a modest selection of smaller works, many of them portrait busts, placed about the galleries. Many Cleveland sculptors worked for local firms, supplying architectural decoration. Some also taught in area schools. But whatever their vocations, the sculptors who worked on a large scale were obliged to assemble equipment and to put in many hours of risky preparation if they wished to see their ideas materialize. To ease the burden, the May Show accepted finished models in lieu of the actual works themselves.

Alexander Blazys, a Russian expatriate, submitted (1927) a bronze figure group entitled *City Fettering Nature*. This symbolic monument—the only May Show sculpture on permanent display at the Museum (with an ambitious size and thematic presentation)—marked the apogee of major sculpture in Cleveland during the pre-war period.

In post-war years, sculpture took on a markedly different identity. Sculptors moved away from the figure as they sought to exploit the plastic qualities of their medium in new ways. (Figurative elements that remained became- in the sculptors' hands—pretexts for the employment of surface effects).

In the 1950s movement and abstraction became important to Cleveland sculptors. Piling up; cantilevering; mounting on spindly supports; creating open, seemingly weightless structures became one favored *modus operandi*. The small was made large (influenced by the work of artists such as Claes Oldenburg); unusual placement in a gallery was explored, and the geometrically oriented object came into favor. Welded steel also came into its own. By the middle 1960s sculpture could be almost anything that occupied space and, in the case of light sculpture, controlled space much better than the object itself.

With these changes, the problems that the May Show encountered with paintings were minimal compared with those of sculpture. Some works were extremely heavy, while others were oversized. Installers fretted with the problem of mounting irregular shapes according to the artist's wishes. Electrical and mechanical pieces had a dismaying way of breaking down.

In order to cope with unusual and difficult to handle sculptures, the May Show was obliged to set some rules. In the late 1960s limits for weight were established, as well as for size. Electric objects had to prove their dependability through a trial run, and an object's potential for being a bad neighbor in the show was considered in its installation.

Traditional materials are now re-emerging. Objects in bronze, especially, are more in evidence. Craftsmanship, too, as it relates to elegantly defined volumes and finished surfaces, is also regaining some of the prestige it once enjoyed.

Graphics

Graphics is a diverse category that includes drawing, lithography, intaglio printing techniques, silk screening—the product of which is known as a serigraph—and recently developed processes such as xerography. Graphics have enjoyed a surge of popularity in recent decades, in part because of an evolution in public taste.

Urban life styles and the modest finances of many collectors have led to an appreciation for prints and drawings because they are relatively inexpensive and can incorporate virtually any image, quietly or emphatically, within a compact format. Artists have discovered that the printmaking techniques offer them virtually unlimited possibilities, and the prints they make have a high sales potential.

From the 1930s, graphics have been well represented in the May Show. Printmaking was a major art form during the depression years when many artists—especially painters—made prints as an alternative to their main interests. There were dedicated printmakers in Cleveland—like Kalman Kubinyi and the members of a printmakers' club who often used presses installed in the Museum for artists.

In the decade of the 1960s, graphics enjoyed another surge of popularity. It was discovered—or more accurately, rediscovered—that graphics offered broad ranges of possibilities to the imaginative creators. At one extreme was etching, whose history emphasized changes from a select elite toward broader audiences. In essence, there was something for all in graphics: the economy and clarity of shape and flat tones of serigraphs; the rich modulations of etchings; the spontaneity of lithographs; and the three-dimensional qualities of embossing.

Those who sent prints to May Shows and who wished to experiment found that many commercial techniques had been developed—especially in silk screening and lithography—which they could apply in new ways. Screening processes, some used in decorating cloth, were also employed in painting. Images derived from photography also began to appear in surprising contexts during the 1960s. In fact, an entire field of art was beginning to take form under the impact of experimental attitudes

May Show judges (47th May Show, 1965).
Evan Turner, Fairfield Porter, Edward B. Henning.
Photo: Martin Linsey.

and technological developments: an art form in which the work of art was a synthesis of two or more previously separate media.

Recently, artists have turned to papermaking as a further direction in graphics, introducing new materials into the pulp from which the paper is made and casting the pulp as if it were a piece of sculpture. Interest in graphics now remains high. One can predict with some certainty that graphics will continue as a major category in the May Show for years to come, just as the medium has increased in attention and emphasis in other locations throughout the country.

Photography—also a printmaking process—is the most visible and influential plastic medium touching our lives. Until recently, however, it was not strongly represented in the May Show. In the pre-war years photographers in Cleveland and their painter colleagues tended to choose the same sort of subject matter. Then works could be sorted into categories of landscape and figural compositions.

As more versatile photographic equipment became available, however, and as experimental forms of photography became generally known, local photographers began to free themselves from the influence of painting. Close-up photography became popular as did blurred-action shots. Tonal characteristics were adjusted for greater effect, and graininess in the negative—once considered a drawback—was exploited.

Today photography is no longer viewed as something of a poor relative to painting; indeed, it has come to be a prime instrument in determining the painter's approach to subject matter. In recent years this turnaround has been very much in evidence. Any number of painters are now openly and unabashedly relating their paintings to photography.

As for photographs themselves, the modestly-sized prints that have always been a presence in the show are still very much in evidence. In large measure, the prints exhibited tend primarily to explore a poetically evocative mood. However, large prints, color, and serial compositions have also made an appearance.

Crafts

Certain media—like drawing on paper and painting on canvas—have traditionally been labelled as "fine arts" in opposition to crafts. However, more serious thought has recognized that all are art forms; the only question is how much emphasis is put on aesthetic vs. functional qualities. Recently it has been realized that such traditional crafts as pottery, metalwork, and textiles must also be taken as seriously as such "fine arts" as painting and sculpture.

The traditional definition used to separate arts from crafts was based on the notion that the arts are valued for their power to affect our emotional and cognitive responses, while the crafts are generally valued in respect to their usefulness. Crafts have generally been equated with "fine art" when the quality of design and workmanship equals or surpasses function in importance. This brings us back to the May Show, where the crafts exhibited in the early years tended to be either commercially produced or were examples of time-honored traditional forms, many of them introduced by European immigrants.

After a market for crafts developed—spurred on by a willingness to purchase handmade objects in the face of an ever-increasing deluge of machine-made goods, craftsmen were able to make a living outside a factory setting. Many people, their lives shaped by automation and labor-saving devices, became interested in objects made by independent craftsmen. Schools and universities established arts and crafts programs. Teachers found themselves in a favored position with extensive resources at their disposal. They were stimulated by contact with the campus atmosphere as well as with their students and they became a seminal force in the further development of the handmade object.

Early members of this group were Viktor Schreckengost and Kenneth Bates. Schreckengost designed and made commercial pottery, exerted a strong impact on industrial design, and did water colors. He sparked a revival in the direct carving of cer-

May Show registration. Service Entrance,
Cleveland Museum of Art. Photo: Ann Edwards.

ALL ENTRANTS
PAY FEE HERE

amics. In this last endeavor he acted to bring a craft medium to the level approaching fine art. Bates developed enamels of all kinds to the same high level as did John Paul Miller with jewelry and Fred Miller with metalwork. Other teachers like Edris Eckhardt and Elsa Vick Shaw, both working primarily in glass in the 1940s and 1950s, made significant contributions toward a highly important aesthetic position for crafts.

Enthusiasm for the crafts had always been strong in Cleveland, now it began to find new channels. Edris Eckhardt, working in glass, rediscovered in the 1950s the procedure for creating shimmering layers of gold leaf—a technique not widely used since Roman times. Kenneth Bates brought such techniques as *plique a jour* to a high level of quality in enameling and John Paul Miller developed the ancient method of granulation in goldsmithing to an incredible level of artistry. The crafts of other cultures were also explored. The potter Toshiko Takaezu, an American of Oriental lineage, brought to the Institute of Art her knowledge of Japanese ceramics. She communicated an approach to pottery that united a reverence for the traditions of the craft with a sensitivity to new forms.

By the early sixties, traditional barriers between crafts and fine arts had all but disappeared in Cleveland. Ideas were exchanged across an ever-narrowing divide. Sculptors tried their hands at pottery, while potters applied to their work concepts of assemblage, decaling, and creating sculptures.

Weaving, which in earlier May Shows appeared primarily in a functional guise, expanded to the limits of its definition as an art form. In fact, the medium is taking so many new directions—particularly moving toward sculpture—that it is coming to be known as fiber forms.

Glass in recent decades has also become important. Its development as a medium owes a great deal to schools and universities which provide the resources necessary for blowing and casting. Expensive kilns and specialized equipment are needed for glassmaking, and the artists have been quick to take advantage of such new equipment. Most of them are to be found working close to the educational establishment or on a cooperative basis with commercial glassblowing firms.

Jewelry and metalworking have also been traditionally strong in Cleveland. The Institute of Art has, from its earliest years, held classes in these media. Before the Second World War, the two most important names in jewelry and metalworking were John Burton and Anna Hill. Since the war, two names have predominated—Frederick Miller and John Paul Miller.

In its complexity—in the skills required, and in the value of the materials employed—working in precious metals is—like jewel-cutting—one of the premier crafts. Since the technique is so complex and expensive, it has undergone fewer basic changes than other crafts. Its approach has been evolutionary and much enriched by examples of adornments in other cultures.

Conclusion

Through its support of the May Show since 1919, The Cleveland Museum of Art has brought attention to numerous artists from the northeastern Ohio region. The show has had a compelling appeal to area artists since it has given them the opportunity to show their works and to be judged with their peers on a regional basis. The May Show has served as a model of the interaction between a major museum and its local artists, providing a showcase and a means to stimulate artistic growth in various media in this section of the United States.

Jay Hoffman
Instructor, Department of Art History & Education

Biographies

The biographies of only nine artists who regularly contributed to past May Shows can scarcely do justice to the many regional artists who enthusiastically exhibited at the Museum over the years. Instead, these capsule statements should be seen as a start toward the compilation of information on many other painters, sculptors, and craftsmen who made a lasting contribution to artistic activity in northeastern Ohio. These nine artists should also be seen as symbolic figures who provide valuable insight into the ways in which some May Show participants were trained and how they reacted to trends in the art world. Often, they were influenced by regional interests: their immediate friends or environment—urban or country—thereby providing an accurate historical picture of changing taste at a given moment in time. By studying their life and work it is possible to see the May Show in a new light - one that permits a deeper understanding of the traditions and origins of local artists who were consistently collected and applauded by an art audience in Cleveland.

GPW

Kenneth Francis Bates (born 1904)

Kenneth Bates, master enamelist, articulate author, and distinguished professor, came to Cleveland in 1927. A graduate of the Massachusetts School of Art, he joined the faculty of Cleveland Art School at the invitation of its director, Henry Turner Bailey. During his years of service as teacher and head of the design department, Bates wrote on enameling techniques and the principles of design. Artistically, his own work encompassed a wide variety of techniques and themes; his enamels consistently won prizes in the May Show for their design and execution.

An avid horticulturist, Bates seeks inspiration from flowers and plant life. Childhood fascination with wild blossoms mirrored in the transparent rivulets of a pond near his home fostered a life-long enchantment with nature. His personal interpretations of nature's diverse shapes, forms, colors, and textures range from realistic renderings to stylizations influenced by synthetic cubism and abstraction.

Color—vitally important for the enamelist—is found everywhere in the garden. Stimulated by the sharp unexpected accents of a flower's center or by the more subtle variations at the tips of its petals, Bates chooses from an infinite array of hues. With changing nuances he creates such effects as deep water, textures of foliage, and patterns of frost. The representational rendering, *Butterflies and Thistle,* has an iridescent quality that gives it a many-colored appearance when light rays cross its surface. *Late August,* a two-foot enamel panel, has sharp accents of ruby on gold which make this work an abstract conception of the garden in a final burst of color.

As a medium, enamel is especially suited for abstract interpretations. A molten substance which is flowing, changing, and fusing, it easily creates illusions. Different techniques allow for endless variations, reproducing a wide range of visual effects. Bates explored some of these possibilities in *Somber Depths Within.* The simple organic design floats on a glossy dark ground. Wells of imagery and fantasy are revealed in the gold luster delicately crackled over a swirl of opaque red enamel.

Although an enamelist is usually restricted to a flat, two-dimensional surface (as in the works noted above), he is frequently inspired by the three-dimensional manifestations of nature. The graceful curves of a rosebud or the trumpeting petals of the lily are points of departure for Bates. He often uses a form suggested by the poppy-seed pod as an elegant knob or finial for covered bowls. Three-dimensional design becomes especially important in fashioning forged or hammered pieces of jewelry which are embellished with enamel.

A new area of experimentation in construction with hammered rough-edged forms arose when Bates began using a welding torch. Applied to copper sheets, the torch fuses molten pieces of metal, creating rippled edges and burning holes. Enamel is then added to the surface where desired. *Sycamore Bark* employs this technique to capture the rugged texture of the tree's outer crust, deftly combining crudeness with sparkle and polish.

For additional contrast, Bates occasionally incorporates different materials and unusual objects with enamel. Intarsia—the combining of inlaid wood with another medium—was employed in the large mural he designed for the Campus Sweater Building on Euclid Avenue. Fitted together like a giant jigsaw puzzle, this composition balances walnut wood with vitreous enamel-on-copper areas. Interesting contrast is also produced by the close juxtapositions of enamel and bits of rusted iron or other objects found on Bates's backyard beach. The inclusion of weather-beaten forms with precious materials enriches the tactile quality of the surface by placing coarse textures next to smooth ones.

Other than enamels based on themes from nature, Bates has frequently exhibited religious designs in the May Show. Impressed by French ecclesiastic art while studying at the Fontainebleau School of Fine Arts (1927), he uses decorative panels and crosses relating closely to the spirit of the church. A number of these works have Early Christian or Byzantine iconography. *Festival in Byzantium,* a twelve-by-eighteen-inch panel, is inspired by traditional motifs of the Byzantine period.

Bates also uses *plique-a-jour,* a form of transparent enameling, to imitate the appearance of stained glass. The vigil light created for the altar of the Roman Catholic Chapel in the National Naval Medical Center, Bethesda, Maryland, employs this technique. A balanced effect of richness and simplicity is achieved in the five-inch-high circular construction. Two of the six panels are embellished with silver crosses. Accompanying design motifs set with *plique-a-jour* enamel produce a jewel-like radiance when the lamp is lit.

One work created by Bates for the May Show is a gold enamel box containing gold and resting on a base of solid ebony polished to a satiny patina. The box received a special award for excellence in craftsmanship. A complex variety of panels and cantilevers depict artistic masterpieces and scenes from the Museum and the Institute of Art. Objects from the Guelph Treasures, Rodin's *Thinker,* and a miniature version of Matisse's *Fete de Fleurs* decorate some of the panels. Others show pottery-making, portrait-painting, and fir trees representing the Museum's past Christmas-caroling services. Executed in *cloisonné,* the panels use fine gold wire to form the outlines of the design, blocking one color from another. The resulting cells are filled in with red, blue, black, and white enamel. For brilliance, minute pieces of metal foil were added to shine through the transparent glaze. The Trustees of The Cleveland Museum of Art and the Cleveland Institute of Art commissioned the box for presentation to a distinguished area art patron.

Throughout his career, Bates has maintained a level of excellence equalled only by the creative energy with which he works. Interest in the study of design revealed in natural phenomena has been a primary source of inspiration. Many techniques have been used to demonstrate the vast possibilities in decorative enamel for brilliant color, intricate design, and fanciful fairy-tale effects. Enthusiastically searching for ways to expand his visual horizons, Kenneth Bates has never lost the excitement generated by the first piece to come from his kiln.

August F. Biehle (born 1885)

August Biehle, native Clevelander, trained as an apprentice decorator with his father at Rohrheimer Brooks Inc. His father was a master decorator brought over from Germany to paint meticulous designs and floral motifs for nineteenth-century mansions. Several of the Biehles' decorating assignments were on "Millionaire's Row"—Euclid Avenue, at that time—including the Hanna mansion. Later, August Biehle worked with his father at the Biehle Brothers decorating firm, doing the interior of the Glamorgan mansion in Alliance. While it is now the administrative offices for the Board of Education, there are still remnants of the painted designs visible in the basement rathskeller.

Decorating was not his only art training, for in 1903 Biehle went to Europe with two art students—William Finkelstein (Zorach) and Dave Brubeck. In France he took a life-drawing class and studied the work of Corot in the Louvre. Because of his German heritage and ability to speak the language, Biehle moved on to Munich where he remained for two years. There he attended the Kunst Gewerbe Schule—a school for designers. Doing numerous sketches of the Munich scenery and people and details of flowers and fruits, Biehle developed a distinctive style of flat decorative patterns. His work incorporated the decorative techniques—woodgraining and stippling—as had George Braque's, whose father also was a decorator.

When Biehle returned to Cleveland (1905) he worked as a decorator; by 1908 he had formed his own company decorating theaters and residences in Youngstown. Working at Sherwin Williams for two years as a color artist, Biehle was then able to finance a return trip to Munich for further study. From the Kunst Gewerbe Schule he passed the entrance examination for the Fine Arts Royal Academy. There he studied under Angelo Jack and Julius Dietz who, as Biehle said "were the famous ones, but I learned more from a lot nobody ever heard of. . . ." Contemporary European movements—The Blue Rider, German Expressionism, and the French Fauves—influenced his painting:

the broad brush strokes, spontaneous romantic sentiments, and similar compositional movements are evident.

In 1912 Biehle returned to Cleveland's Sherwin Williams decorator department as a demonstrator, working on sample color charts and wall samples. At this time, wallpaper became the vogue, virtually eliminating decorator painting. A new career as an apprentice lithographer with Otis Lithograph (later Continental Lithograph) began in 1913. Known as a "black" artist, Biehle did the fundamental reproduction drawing on a lithographic stone with a black wax pencil. Until his retirement in 1952, he produced most of his lithography for theater marquees, circus posters, and billboard ads.

Despite his obligations at Otis Lithograph, Biehle continued to paint landscapes, still lifes, and portraits. His paintings were regularly selected for the May Show, where they frequently earned prizes—one of which was presented in the 1920's by the noted artist George Bellows. Biehle's continual contribution to the May Show was recognized when The Cleveland Museum of Art granted him an Emeritus Non-Jury Entrant status. After participating in twenty-five May Shows, Biehle attained the privilege of exhibiting in the May Show without the element of competition.

Always a student of painting, Biehle studied with Henry G. Keller in an informal group labeled the "Summer School," which gathered at Keller's cottage in Berlin Heights. Occasional classes at the John Huntington Polytechnic Institute (formerly the Cleveland Polytechnic Institute) enabled him to study with his friends Paul Travis and Frank Wilcox. Years of weekends at Brandywine were spent with his co-worker at Otis Lithograph, William Sommer. (In fact, when Sommer died, it was August Biehle who had the responsibility of dividing the paintings from the artist's estate among his children.) He also attended night classes at the Cleveland Institute of Art; the most recent instruction came in 1956 at a summer session at Bowling Green State University with Max Weber.

Just as he studied painting throughout his life, Biehle contin-

ued to participate actively in the Cleveland art world. He designed covers for the *Bystander* and the *Cygnet Monthly,* past Cleveland art magazines. Biehle also designed program covers and posters for the newly-formed Play House. As a member of the Kokoon Art Club, he joined with a cross section of Cleveland's leading artists, musicians, and politicians in a variety of art activities such as masked balls, auctions, exhibits, and classes. But his social involvement also included other interests: he was well-known as a gymnast in the Turnverein and he was a baritone soloist for Catholic and Christian Science churches.

Biehle enriched the romanticism and direct quality of painting begun in Munich with a dominant blue outline. The rugged colorful landscape and shimmering sunlight motifs of Berlin Heights remained in his style as he painted Zoar, Ohio. Located in Tuscarawas County, Zoar was an experiment in communal living; it was settled by Separatists from the Lutheran Church in 1817. Disbanded in 1898, Zoar was the most substantial and enduring of Ohio's communal undertakings. The first of Biehle's several trips there was in 1920. The flour mill, the brewery, the first red-tile roofed house, and the shady roads of Zoar were represented in lyrical paintings, reminiscent of Vincent Van Gogh. Often opaque and transparent water colors were mixed with crayon and pencil drawing to express his own poetic sensibilities.

Never content with one style or doctrine, Biehle also did abstractions in contrast to his realistic landscapes. These compositions transformed decorative shapes by superimposing a rhythmic baroque line movement. Among these abstractions was a series of frosted windowpanes. The subtly balanced colors, intricate patterns, and delicate lines appear to indicate a mystic meaning behind these frosted images.

Besides realism and abstraction, Biehle did murals for public schools (under the W. P. A. program) and decorated a number of private enterprises. With the help of Frank Meyer, Herman Petersen, and others, he was responsible for twenty-seven murals at the Alpine Village (a former Cleveland restaurant) representing highlights of well-known operas. Biehle's desire for accuracy required extensive research on the settings and costumes of these operas. Less study was required for the twelve murals decorating two rooms at the Hofbrau Haus, another Cleveland restaurant.

The murals—landscapes of Ohio scenery, poignant portraits, still lifes, flowers, and expressive decorative paintings—exhibit not only a variation in subject matter but also in technique. Classifying himself as "essentially a decorative painter," Biehle depends on his draftsmanship regardless of the particular style. The carry-overs from his early training also remain: exaggerated significance of contour, colors not completely modulated, and dynamic rhythmic movement. The versatility of these stylistic achievements is paralleled by his long and productive painting career. Winning the award for outstanding contribution to the Fine Arts of Parma (1976), August Biehle was once again recognized for his dominant participation in the Greater Cleveland art scene and the May Show.

Shirley Aley Campbell (born 1925)

Shirley Aley Campbell is a renowned figurative painter whose paintings have expanded in various media, subject matter, size, and technique. A Cleveland native, she graduated from the Cleveland Institute of Art in 1947, receiving the Agnes Gund Scholarship. After painting and living in Puerto Rico for a year, she moved to New York and worked as a commercial artist for Charles Brackett and Associates. In 1951 Campbell returned to Cleveland where she was employed as a commercial artist for one year at Lou Federman and Associates.

It was in Cleveland during the years 1955-1959 that Campbell developed her Puerto Rican Period, reflecting wistful, undernourished children. A particularly compassionate painting of this style, entitled *Requiem for Dominic,* was a prizewinner in the 1957 May Show. The strong emotions of a funeral procession were portrayed by the large-eyed expressions of the city children. Working in traditional water color, tempera, and pen, Campbell typified the souls of children, their sorrows, and their childhood joys. Another painting of this style (*Metamorphosis*) was selected for the New York Armory Show "Art, U.S.A., 1959."

The sensitive Puerto Rican statements of human conditions were preserved in her Civil Rights paintings (1960-64). Topics of discrimination, equal rights, and the death of the Reverend Bruce Klunder in Cleveland became powerful painted subjects. Figures were distorted and abstracted to a greater degree, and titles were used for an expression of awareness. These representations of social consciousness symbolized Campbell's perception of world conditions at the time.

Using painting as a "means of establishing communications with one's fellowman" continued in the Burlesque Period (1965-69). In meeting the owner of the Cleveland Roxy Theater Limited—when on the same radio program—Campbell became interested in the possibility of expressing burlesque's fading years. Over 500 sketches of dressing tables, corridors, musicians, and burlesque queens of Cleveland, Toledo, and Washington were done in less than a year. The burlesque queens' rolls of fat, sagging flesh, and poses of exhaustion relate to Ivan Albright's treatment of the figure. The compositions were originally thought of as arrangements of abstract forms which permitted either the entire figure or part of it to emerge. There was an exaggeration of reality through the combination of several people for personal expressions of humanization rather than for the glorification of burlesque.

Powerful psychological declarations of estrangement and alienation of burlesque queens were extended into a short-lived Derelict Period (1969-70). The eerie theatrical light of burlesque was now aimed at the lowest section of society. The faint prospects and future of these characters reveal the frailties of all men. The harsh effects of dissipation, degradation, and rejection were factually recorded.

Working principally in acrylic paint, Campbell began her current Realist Period in 1970. While the subject matter was varied, most works ranged in size from 5 feet by 7 feet to 5 feet by 9 feet. Among portraits of her family and friends is *Five Figure Exercise—Opus I* (1970, owned by the Butler Institute of American Art). Representing the most influential people of her life, it is also a statement of prominent local personalities. From the left is Leon Gordon Miller, an industrial designer; Joseph Green Butler, director of the Butler Institute of American Art; Dr. Lawrence Vincent, chairman of the humanities department at Cuyahoga Community College, Western Campus; Eugenia Thornton Silver, literary critic; and John Puskas, Cleveland enamelist and a May Show participant.

Campbell's portrait of *Art Deco and the World of Bernice Kent* was in the 1971 May Show. Bernice Kent, a lecturer and collector of Art Deco and Art Nouveau, was depicted in a 1902 black velvet knickers suit. The flamboyancy of the Art Deco period is reiterated by this symbolic icon.

A later series of paintings depicts the bygone days of the Cleveland amusement park, Euclid Beach. An empty roller coaster, a former top banana with a burlesque queen, and a clown with a contemporary youth are combined to present a ghostly aura of this lost pleasure center. This series was Campbell's first major surrealist work, "the theme being the demise of both Euclid Beach and burlesque."

Currently, Campbell is painting noted political personalities. She began the series in recognition of women's struggles to achieve political or legal success. Already completed is Common Pleas Judge Ann McManamon, portrayed departing from the Municipal Courtroom and entering Common Pleas Court. This portrait, as others, was conceived by sketching the subject from life.

Campbell's personal painted messages have influenced her students, fellow artists, and the May Show contemporary art scene.

Herbert Carroll Cassill (born 1928)

Born in Percival, Iowa, Carroll Cassill's first interest in the arts came from an older brother who had studied painting with Grant Wood, among others. As a student at the State University of Iowa he was introduced to printmaking by Mauricio Lasansky, and under his guidance Cassill earned both his B.F.A. (1948) and M.F.A. (1950). He reflected Lasansky's belief in a "new direction" for printmaking. The synthesis of the intaglio techniques of line engraving, drypoint, and soft-ground etching became meaningful to Cassill only within "the context of the involvement with the whole process of making the print." Thus, identification of different processes is subservient to the image of the print itself. Cassill's appreciation for the inherent qualities of intaglio prevent his consistently meticulous craftsmanship from being impaired by preoccupation with technique at the expense of communication.

Two prints done while Cassill was a student are significant for their indications of his later developments. *The Sophisticate,* a satirical intaglio print, is often cited as Cassill's first important print (1948). The horn-rimmed glasses, the distant stage lights, and the "flute-necktie" together portray a critical comment on those people who removed themselves from society. The print ("the etching") was in part a happy accident resulting from leaving the plate in the acid too long. Regardless of its origin, the dynamic sharp lines against the soft, dusty texture produce a powerful visual statement. *The Paper Bird* (1950) was done as a declaration of commitment as a printmaker. It is unusual because it was produced in color intaglio, whereas most of Cassill's works are expressive variations of black and white. His preference for black and white prints relates to the desire for a social statement which he finds in the earliest Western prints and in a "continually thriving" tradition of printmaking.

In 1948, as a graduation present to himself, Cassill went to Mexico. The enjoyment of this initial exposure led to many return visits. Inspired by his observations of the Mexican bullfights and the prints of Goya, he developed works such as *Toro* (1959). The black masses of the bull were contrasted with the linear background to form a strong tension. Cassill continued these bullfight images, as well as other motifs, when he was appointed an instructor of printmaking at his alma mater (1953). It was also in 1953 that Cassill was awarded the coveted Tiffany Fellowship in Prints.

Cassill moved to Cleveland in 1957 to head the printmaking department at the Cleveland Institute of Art. Participating in the May Show, he won a special award for an intaglio entitled *Icarus* (1958). Cassill's print of the falling figure of Icarus was intended to relate not only to human problems but to the resurrection of the human figure in art. As such, it was a statement of Cassill's desire to use significant gestures of the human figure to communicate provocative visual and emotional concepts.

Preoccupation with the human figure continued with *New World and Old* and *To a New World* (1960), two prize-winning prints from the May Show. Both were intaglios which varied in degree of abstraction to produce contemplations of mixed reality and illusion. The intensity of feeling comes from the human relationships within the quizzical, shadowy environments. Both prints were expressions of social consciousness: *New World and Old,* the two different generations; and *To a New World,* the end of a past "dishonest" decade.

In addition to social concerns, Cassill's printing subjects were derived from poetry (for example, *The Apparition of the Other Brother*), family portraits, and subtle comic overtones, as in the *Square Tree.* Each of these prints have a master craftsmanship and a particular artistic vision that pursue evocative images. Cassill states that he was influenced and inspired by the prints of Rembrandt, Goya, Lasansky, and the eighteenth-century Japanese artist Sharaku. Yet there is no intention to imitate these artists' images in his own work. As an added note, it seems fitting that the majority of Cassill's prints inspired by literature were "pulled" from a ton-and-a-half press once owned by the renowned printer Leblanc.

In 1966 The Cleveland Museum of Art held an unusual exhibition entitled "Printmaking—A Family Affair." It provided the opportunity to view Carroll Cassill's work along with that of his wife and two children. An accomplished printmaker and student of Lasansky, Jean Kubota Cassill has produced prints of misty landscapes with delicate, peaceful images.

For recognition of his philosophical images and personal technique, Carroll Cassill was the first printmaker and the eleventh Cleveland artist to receive the Visual Arts Award of the Women's City Club (1971). The award was also an acknowledgment of his participation in an abundant number of regional and national exhibitions, including the Library of Congress Print Annual, the Boston Printmakers' Annual, the Print Club of Philadelphia, and, of course, the May Show. Recognizing that the May Show is a "unique show which puts emphasis on the better possibilities of regional art," Cassill also believes that the level of skill has improved among the entrants.

Besides being an effective, productive artist, Cassill is deeply involved with his students at the Cleveland Institute of Art. Urging his students to be inventive and yet to communicate a message, Cassill believes that "one could not hope to be sensitive to the problems and aspirations of the student with only a theoretical understanding of art." Cassill's current printmaking project involves the recurrent theme of finding his family past—"resolving a social contract," he says.

While Cassill does occasional water colors, it is the reflective, quiet intensity of his prints which have been an inspiration to his students and fellow artists.

John Clague (born 1928)

John Clague, talented sculptor and experienced art instructor, has exhibited many works in the Cleveland May Show. The stylistic development of his career can be traced from the early figurative *Unicyclists* (shown in 1955) through blossom motifs and planar abstractions to current kinetic structures which produce musical sounds. He is now exploring the expressive possibilities of scored steel surfaces contrasted with flat-black paint.

Artistic proficiency appeared early in Clague's career; while he was still in high school his work won several national prizes as well as local awards. Receiving a scholarship, he attended the Cleveland Institute of Art where he majored in painting through his senior year and studied as a graduate student under William McVey. In 1955, still a student, Clague entered the sculpture entitled *Unicyclists* in the May Show. The early figurative work is modeled in sculpt-metal, a pliable medium which hardens like metal when dry. This readily available substance temporarily satisfied Clague's yearning for spatial freedom which was fully realized in welded structures. A humorous and playful air enhance the cunningly balanced composition.

In addition to working with figurative themes, Clague consistently seeks inspiration from the observation of other organic forms. Water-smoothed stones, turtles, frogs, and plants reveal a beauty based on the principles of discipline and order. One series of sculptures—derived from blossom motifs—explores the process of growth expressed through the elastic energy of planes. Erupting from bases like sprouts from the earth, these forms branch out in several directions. The sequential existence of planes in time and space represent growth, while life's dramas and conflicts are mirrored in the number and diversity of the forms. *The Flower of Erebus,* exhibited in the 1960 May Show, is a nine-foot-tall steel and bronze sculpture from this series. Named for the Greek mythological land of darkness under the earth through which the dead pass before entering Hades, this work powerfully dominates space. Energy is menacingly focused in the spiky petal forms rising above the viewer.

Continued experimentation with the sculptural possibilities of fixed and moving planes in space opened another avenue of creativity for Clague. Blossom motifs were followed by non-representational planar progressions. Combined with slabs of sheet steel or fiberglass, the introduction of paint in these works allowed Clague to explore the sculptural interplay of sharply defined color patterns upon equally well-defined shapes. Rigidly controlled application of these patterns produced in-and-out visual images which changed the rectangular shapes and the directions of the angled planes. Color provided the necessary stabilization which permitted Clague to extend the number and diversity of visual experiences united in a single structure.

Progression in Black and White, completed in 1963 (the second of this planar series) represents a total effect that is totem-like; it can be read as a total configuration—a whole containing parts. The use of titles like "Progression" and "Overture" imply a part of the visual effect. These abstractions are tangible equivalents of musical situations. The sculpture is constructed from a series of themes and variations to be read through space and time. The profiles of the disks and slabs change greatly as one walks around the structure. At first limiting his color patterns to black and white, Clague later used different hues as an even more subtle and varied means of suggesting movement and displacement.

In 1969, Clague's work made a transition from immobile planar abstractions which suggested motion to kinetic structures which did move. These new sculptures also shifted from implying musical situations to actually producing musical sounds. In these works, long vertical stems and panels rise from a spherical section base. When set in motion the rocking energy of the base causes the assembled vertical shapes to interact, resulting in a variety of sounds. The relationship between movement and musical sound is a characteristic feature of twentieth-century sculpture.

Auriculum I is an offshoot of Clague's kinetic series. This gleaming stainless steel sculpture stands twenty feet tall on the terrace of the Research Library of Ohio's Ashland College. Commissioned by the college, it is neither the monument to founding fathers nor the rigid status symbol that one might expect; it was built for the students. Mechanically involving a complex system of pendulums suspended from gimbals, the structure is precision-ground like a giant compass. Activated by the physical participation of the viewer or, on a gusty day, by the wind, the motion of the large pendulum produces a rocking or rotating movement. This in turn stimulates a second smaller pendulum in the upper reaches of the sculpture which swings in the opposite direction. Combined, these motions cause the suspended rods to interact with a spray of stainless steel planes. At the same time, other strikers play upon the six petal-like forms which radiate from the sculpture's central axis. Varying pitches and resonances are produced in bell-like tones.

Clague had begun working on the model for *Auriculum I* before receiving the actual commission from Ashland College. By coincidence, his design corresponded beautifully to the library site. The four twelve-foot legs relate to the library's four-sided terrace, and the six petals overhead reflect the hexagonal tower. With the basic shape of an X, *Auriculum I* matches the motif of the building frieze designed by William McVey. While at rest, the sculpture's symmetry corresponds to the formality of the site; when placed in motion, its sound and visual excitement echo the vitality of the students.

Inspired by the beauty of *Auriculum's* ground and burnished steel plates, Clague has begun a new series. Combining the reflectability of steel with a flat-black paint, he has achieved some interesting effects. Although the work remains two-dimensional, the polished steel seems to undulate—projecting an illusionary third dimension. Also, the steel surface reflects the surrounding color, changing character with each corresponding change in atmosphere.

Clague's career has been divided into generations; various periods explore representational forms, kinetic sculptures, sound-producing works, and polished steel surfaces. Overall, he has treated nature's inspiration with authority, continually striving for a totally individual expression of beauty. In his hands, steel bars leap and dance, painted forms become calligraphy in space, and kinetic works express a visual harmony of movement and sound.

Edris Eckhardt (born 1907)

Edris Eckhardt, a native of Cleveland, is internationally known for her ceramic and glass sculptures. As a young student, she attended Saturday morning classes at The Cleveland Museum of Art where she became interested in working with clay. Later, an office job with the decorators Palmer and Riley exposed her to the beauty around her and led her to enter the Cleveland Institute of Art. She was awarded a scholarship and was eventually able to quit her job and devote full attention to her studies.

After several years of post-graduate study, Eckhardt took a small studio and began working in clay. Henry Keller visited her studio and advised her to learn more about glazes. Almost without realizing it, she had been working smaller and finer, demonstrating her interest in ceramic sculpture.

Working with clay appealed to her; it was a medium where art and commercial success met without conflict. It was much easier to earn one's living selling small ceramics, priced in line with a middle-class income, rather than large-scale bronze figures which cost several hundred dollars to cast. In addition, the pastel shades and new color combinations of ceramic glazes were better suited to the new homes than heavy bronze pieces.

Some of Eckhardt's most popular ceramic sculptures were inspired by children's stories. Works based on characters from fairy tales and nursery rhymes, many of which were exhibited in Cleveland May Shows, were well received by the general public. The sculptures were sold as quickly as they could be made.

In addition to children's literature, animals also served as an inspiration for Eckhardt. During the 1940's her pensive pups, hectic horses, and galloping gazelles were made into pins decorating wartime wardrobes. Jewelry added a touch of wit to the otherwise sober fashions which were chosen with an eye for durability rather than style. Unequalled by any assembly-line product, each pin possessed a distinctive character. Eckhardt personally created each pin from the original model through the firing, glazing, and painting. This was partially a necessity-born virtue as it was almost impossible to get anyone to help.

Particularly attractive to the buying public was a new metal-like glaze, developed by Eckhardt, which gave the effect of gold leaf without using an ounce of that precious metal or getting in the way of any wartime shortage. This metallic glaze was often used in combination with white and pastel glazes, forming an interesting contrast. Eckhardt also varied her designs with the seasons; fall fashions were fairly ornate and rich, while spring's designs were fresher and more delicate.

In addition to these whimsical ventures in the fashion world, Eckhardt has also done several more elaborate figurative works. These are likely to be inspired by her mood of the moment. A particularly sensitive clown face, entitled *Painted Mask,* was exhibited in the 1947 May Show. Traditionally a happy subject, the clown was portrayed by Miss Eckhardt with a note of sadness. Even the broad painted smile does not relieve the melancholy air which surrounds the work. *Painted Mask* represents the dual nature of humanity: the front which people present to the world and their inner soul.

Besides her accomplishments in ceramics, Eckhardt has done extensive research in glass. In 1953 she rediscovered the art of fusing gold leaf between sheets of glass to produce the first-known examples of gold glass in almost two thousand years. Originally this technique had been perfected by the Egyptians, who used it for the bottoms of bowls, plates, and cups, as well as for jewelry. The formula disappeared in the Early Christian era and recent attempts to rediscover the technique had failed.

Eckhardt began her search by using only the materials known to the ancient Egyptians, and was greatly surprised when one of her first attempts produced a perfect chunk of gold glass. Unfortunately, she had neglected to keep accurate records of the quantities, firing temperatures, and the rates of heating and cooling. It took a thousand, more carefully documented experiments to produce another piece of gold glass.

Since this rediscovery, Eckhardt has gone beyond the comparatively simple examples of the past in which two sheets of glass encased a gold engraving. Her pieces are built up of ten or more layers of glass with intervening layers of drawing on thin gold or silver tissues. Fixed together, these layers fuse into a solid form about one-eighth to one-fourth of an inch thick. The resulting plaques possess a radiant glow of color and a strong three-dimensional effect.

Following her work with gold glass, Eckhardt experimented with multiple laminations of sheet glass, using layers of enamels, foils, glass lumps, or plant materials to add variety to the substance. She has embedded pieces of glass in abstract bronze reliefs to produce rich textured surfaces. She has also invented a special tool which enables her to draw in molten glass.

Combining these individual techniques with her previous training as a sculptor, Eckhardt has devised special molds for casting free-standing figurative sculptures by the lost-wax method. Made of gypsum, these molds allow for a great expansion and contraction of molten glass and can be put directly into the kiln. The emerging sculpture has a seamless surface and needs no grinding or finishing. Another advantage to this process is that the cost of a gypsum mold is considerably less expensive than the metal molds used in commercial glass casting.

Edris Eckhardt's contributions in the field of glass have been recognized through Guggenheim Fellowships—awarded in 1956 and 1959 for studies in glass—and a Louis Comfort Tiffany Fellowship—awarded in 1959 for designs in stained glass. Her glass and ceramic sculptures have won numerous regional, national, and international awards. Currently her works are in museum collections all over the world.

William M. McVey (born 1906)

William McVey is a well-known art instructor and May Show luminary. He was born in Boston and came to Cleveland as a youth in 1919. McVey entered the Cleveland Institute of Art in 1922, but left a year later when he won a football scholarship to the University of Texas. While playing football in Houston, McVey received the John Heisman trophy for athletic ability. Planning to pursue a career in sports cartooning, he returned to the Cleveland Institute of Art, where he soon became involved in making sculpture.

After graduating in 1928, McVey gained further experience carving cemetery monuments for the Gandola Brothers Company in Cleveland. Finally, with the financial help of a generous Cleveland art patron who established a scholarship fund, McVey went to Paris. There he studied at several French academies; he also worked under Charles Despiau, a well-known sculptor.

McVey's first major success came when the portrait bust of a Texas friend was accepted for the Honor Court at the Paris Salon (1930). Since that time, portrait busts have remained a specialty. His sitters have included his wife, Leza, and fellow artists Clarence Carter and Geoffrey Landsman, as well as many prominent businessmen of the Cleveland area. One of McVey's most life-like busts is of Artur Rodzinski, formerly a conductor of The Cleveland Orchestra. Measurements for this bust were so accurate that the musician's eyeglasses fit the stone face perfectly.

During the Depression, McVey worked on several art projects funded by the government. As part of a program to stimulate the economy, people were given ten week's work in the profession for which they had been trained. McVey carved a grizzly bear from a three-ton granite block, ably capturing the furry bulk of the creature. Originally designed for the old bear pit in Wade Park, this sculpture has since been moved to the Cleveland Zoo.

McVey also received a commission from the Public Works Art Project for a figure to be placed in the Rose Garden in Wade

Park. Later loaned to the Great Lakes Exposition of 1936 for the Horticultural Gardens, *Awakening* is a female figure sculpted from a five-ton block of Georgia marble. Lost in dreams, the form's contours hardly emerge from the block.

McVey's career as a sculptor was interrupted for a few years by World War II. Enlisting as an army private, he was soon using his artistic talent in a combat-recognition training program. He taught drawing to servicemen, enabling them to identify enemy ships and to estimate their tonnage accurately. For this course McVey wrote his own textbook, which became a standard one used by the Air Force for many years.

After the war McVey was able to turn his full attention to creating and teaching art. One of his best-known post-war works is a monument to Winston Churchill. This nine-foot bronze sculpture was commissioned by the Washington Branch of the English Speaking Union to be placed astride the boundary lines of the property of the British Embassy and the District of Columbia as a symbol of Anglo-American unity. McVey's design had been chosen from those of six other sculptors who had submitted models. Working from more than three hundred pictures of Churchill, McVey portrayed him as the statesman of World War II in a business suit, giving his famous victory sign.

In completing the full-scale sculpture, McVey's hardest task was pleasing the English Speaking Union. Some committee members criticized the rough surface texture, claiming that the creases in the bronze suit detracted from the over-all effect. McVey, however, insisted that the rich texture revealed Churchill's dynamic spirit by catching the light and making the surface vibrate.

An even greater amount of controversy centered around the cigar held in Churchill's left hand. While McVey viewed it as an integral part of the design, repeating the "V" of the other hand, the English Speaking Union wanted the cigar removed. Committee members cited the need for formality in an official work, maintaining that although current generations might remember Churchill as a man who smoked cigars, history would associate

him with inspiration and statesmanship. In the end McVey's arguments won out and the cigar was included.

Many of McVey's sculptures were commissioned as public monuments glorifying a vigorous hero or an historical event. These works are often massive in size: the San Jacinto Monument in Texas, for example, is over 550 feet tall. Erected on the San Jacinto battlefield, this monument marks General Sam Houston's victory over the Mexican Army in 1836. Other large-scale monuments have portrayed legendary heroes like Davy Crockett and Paul Bunyan.

Occasionally, McVey's sculptures have architectural overtones; the enclosing of space becomes a vital concern. *Beached Whale* was designed for a shopping center in Urbana near the University of Illinois. Made of cement and marble chips on a welded steel-mesh frame, the whale stretches sixteen feet from stem to stern. Purposely structured to occupy and entertain shoppers' children, the gaping mouth of the whale opens on a jungle-gym crawl-through space. Delighted youngsters become involved in the spatial definition of the work.

McVey's works have been exhibited widely—especially in the Cleveland and Texas areas. Many of his sculptures adorn public buildings throughout the area. McVey has also influenced a great many Cleveland area artists as an instructor at the Cleveland Institute of Art.

Viktor Schreckengost (born 1906)

Viktor Schreckengost, dedicated teacher and perennial May Show exhibitor, has won numerous awards for his artistic endeavors. The multi-faceted record of his accomplishments reaches into the fields of painting, sculpture, ceramics, and industrial design. Born into a generations-long tradition of potters in Sebring, Ohio he has combined a draftsman's skill with a feeling and understanding for form and structure.

Schreckengost's sculpture reflects both the cultural changes of the times and his own artistic evolution. Whimsical ceramic figures have delighted May Show audiences with their infectious humor and gentle satire. *The Dictator* satirizes the robust figure of the Roman Emperor, Nero, who is serenely playing his lyre while a stylized British lion sleeps at his feet. Small figures of Hitler, Mussolini, Stalin, and Hirohito cling in cherub-like fashion to the emperor's chair—a forecast of history. Works like this served as an antidote to the worries of the Depression and were Schreckengost's personal response to the earnestness of traditional art shows and museum competitions.

Regarding ceramics as a fine art and not as a handicraft, Schreckengost developed a special method of working with clay, where forms were cut from a large solid mass of clay instead of being thrown on a potter's wheel or built from coils. Departing from the standard circular forms, Schreckengost created square shapes with angular lines that are modern in design but still retained a basic, primitive appearance. Freed from dictated utilitarian shapes, his pieces became independent sculptural forms as well as containers.

The hewn method opened a new area of interest in architectural sculpture. Reviving the ancient Babylonian practice of adorning buildings with brilliant glazed reliefs, Schreckengost designed several decorative murals for buildings at the Cleveland Zoo. Five large plaques mounted on the towering chimney of the bird building transformed the smokestack into a handsome architectural member. Relating his design to the function of the building, Schreckengost traced the evolution of the bird from its prehistoric ancestors to the American Eagle. Terra cotta was combined with brilliant pieces of colored glass to form an effective contrast with the light grayish-tan brick and sandstone of the building.

Early Settler, done for the Civic Auditorium of Lakewood High School, was modeled in terra cotta and pressed into plaster molds. The towheaded, rawboned Connecticut Yankee with tough buckskin jerkin and rawhide pouch is assembled like a three-dimensional jigsaw puzzle. Interlocking joints, combined with steel and bronze reinforcement rods, made the mural a supporting part of the structure. The clay had been fired at a high temperature, making it more impervious to weather than marble or granite.

Along with his achievements in ceramic sculpture Schreckengost is also recognized for his painting ability. A natural feeling for design, combined with a fresh treatment of materials, lent imagination to his canvases. City-, land-, and seascapes encompass vast panoramas. Working with a mathematician's precision, Schreckengost transformed crowded rows of buildings into quilt-like patterns.

A number of his water colors were developed from quick studies done aboard planes during World War II. Assigned to the visual design section in charge of naval research, Schreckengost's job was to develop three-dimensional terrain models for use in briefing pilots and air crewmen. While flying at high altitudes, he created unique airscapes, turning the large forms of the earth's surface into patterns filled with infinite space. Many of the transparent, flowing water colors were named with descriptive weather-reporting titles. *Cold Front* depicted angry black clouds with the sun's rays showing behind them, while the earth below was seen as somber.

The Second World War also cut off valued European imports; industrial design became increasingly important. Schreckengost continued the involvement with industry which he had begun with the mass production of ceramics in the 1930's, now placing a new emphasis on pure form uncluttered with decoration.

The production process and the practical use of the object became important considerations. As the art director and designer for Murray Ohio Manufacturing Company (makers of juvenile autos, trucks, wagons, and bicycles), Schreckengost worked in close harmony with the production engineering division and the sales department. Bicycles were created with a crisp linear design to economize weight and materials. In manufacturing small cars, legroom, weight, and size were considered; also these vehicles were designed with a low center of gravity to minimize tipping.

In designing dinnerware, the feel of teacup handles and the non-dripping quality of pitcher spouts became important factors. Color combinations were harmonized with table linens and other household articles. Schreckengost, as the chief designer for the American Limoges and Sebring Pottery Companies and the Salem China Company, created pieces with an eye to their proper functions and applied decorations which related to the forms. Grace and simplicity characterized the smooth ovoid shapes of his *Manhattan* pattern. The complete line used approximately sixty decorative treatments, ranging from gay, informal pieces to formal ware. Colored glazes as well as bands of color and stylized flowers created the designs.

As an instructor at the Cleveland Institute of Art, Schreckengost began teaching the principle of industrial design to a few select students. (Later this course blossomed into a full-scale program.) With the expansion of the profession since World War II, his students and influence were found in major industries throughout the nation. Strongly individualistic, Schreckengost consistently continues to seek inventive ways of working with new materials and finding new uses for traditional media.

William Sommer (1867-1949)

William Sommer, or "The Sage of Brandywine," as he was known, was born in Detroit (1867). His early art training consisted of five years of Sunday drawing instructions from Julius Melchers and an apprenticeship at the Calvert Lithograph Company. After becoming a journeyman he worked at his craft for the Bufford Company in Boston, and then in England at Stafford's and Dangerfield Brothers. Sommer's only other academic training came in 1890 when he studied for one year in Munich at Professor Herterich's School of Art. (In the same class was Henry G. Keller, who became an influential force in the Cleveland May Show.) While in Munich, Sommer developed his realism from the use of warm earth colors with highlights of white. Returning to New York (1892), he worked for several lithograph companies specializing in portraits of theatrical performers. It was also in New York that Sommer met his wife, Martha Obermeyer, who became his shield from the problems of the world, enabling him to dedicate himself to his art.

In 1907 Sommer moved to Cleveland to work full time for the Otis Lithograph Company. He lived for seven years in Lakewood, and he helped form the Kokoon Art Club—a sketching club where, at times, Sommer would also lecture. Yet, it was when Sommer moved to Brandywine that he seemed to find his destiny; a one-room schoolhouse became his studio and the rural environment became part of his personality and aspirations. Instead of painting beautiful women, heroic scenes, or allegorical legends, Sommer was inspired by homely rural subjects which could be developed for a universal meaning. In 1918 Sommer designed the settings, costumes, and cover design of the program of *Everyman* produced at the old Play House. He also did the program cover for *The Dumb Messiah* by David Pinksi, one of the first plays devoted to the Zionist movement. In 1919 Sommer began a friendship with Hart Crane, who would later dedicate his poem "Sunday Morning Apples" to Sommer and was the first to introduce Sommer's work in New York.

In 1922 Sommer was accepted in the May Show and by 1924 he had won first prize in freehand drawing. Sommer participated in twenty-six May Shows, receiving three special and twenty other awards. There is no doubt these entries and awards contributed to Sommer's artistic recognition. Sommer's work also hung in seven national museums and he had eighteen one-man shows in American galleries during his lifetime. Yet he seldom, if ever, entered an exhibit; he did not seek publicity or recognition. Instead, friends, gallery directors, or Cleveland Museum of Art officials would visit his studio, picking up any work they could, and then would mount, frame, and enter these pieces themselves. Sommer was only interested in the actual process of creativity, not the exhibition of art works after they were completed.

Once Sommer lost his job (1929) due to the adoption of a more efficient offset press, he turned his full attention to art. The years 1928-1933 are often considered the full flowering of Sommer's art; it is also the period when Cezanne's influence developed into a personal idiom for Sommer. After reading *Since Cezanne* by Clive Bell, Sommer began to develop new ideas of volume and mass, form and structure, and space and composition. By expressing an interest in decoration, coupled with the solidity of construction, swirling forms, and vivacious colors, he produced water colors that took a new direction. While there is no photographic realism of forms, there is a sparkling clarity in the recognition of each form with subjective colors derived from Gauguin.

The fine hardness and clarity of Sommer's drawing is often compared to Ingres. His drawings were often done quickly—preferably with a fountain pen, since it would commit him to a line. Sommer sketched compulsively on whatever was handy, with an accuracy separated from his reason. "Keep your mind out of it" was his advice to striving artists. Often these crisp lines were combined with the subtleties of arbitrary color for rhythmic water while avoiding shading. In fact, Sommer was one of the first Cleveland artists to use the burnt-matchstick method

previously used in Europe. The method consists of an ordinary matchstick slightly softened at the end and then dipped into India ink, simulating a conte or lithographic wax-crayon effect. The technique allows flexibility and movement while maintaining a sense of precision. These linear qualities are often reminiscent of a Japanese calligraphic technique.

Even though the linear qualities of Japanese prints, the rich palette of Gauguin, and the forms of Cezanne can be seen, Sommer was not dominated by any one of these movements, but experimented with them to form his own personal expression. This is also reflected in the portraits of his family and the neighboring Polish Dominski children. The child portraits probe the sad wisdom of youth with expressions of bewilderment and simplicity. Sommer himself thought they were character portraits of the soul, depicting a greater realism than external details.

Sommer also worked in oils, but these are relatively few in number and less spontaneous than his water colors. Throughout these different media and themes, Sommer incorporated his own homespun philosophy: that nature may inspire but the actual creation is the result of the artist's mind.

From 1933-1941 Sommer worked on a number of government projects. Among these were murals for the Cleveland Public Auditorium, the Geneva Post Office, and—perhaps the most famous—a mural for Brett Hall of The Cleveland Public Library. There, Sommer depicted Cleveland Public Square as he envisioned it in 1833. Important themes of religion, law, and culture were symbolized by the Cleveland landmarks of The Old Stone Church, the Court House, and the Academy. In the lower corners are familiar rural animals—a reminder of the extermination of farming life by urban progress. It was also at this time that Sommer designed three murals for the Firestone Tire and Rubber Company building erected at the Chicago World's Fair. These murals inspired Sommer to develop a more massive style with less emphasis on line. While Sommer was not a muralist, the figures appear frozen; there were some difficulties in composing for large spaces.

In 1945 Mrs. Sommer died, leaving William Sommer without his sense of stability. From then to his death in 1949, much of his time was spent in Mormon's Tavern. His ability to handle everyday problems of life was so inadequate that in 1946—upon family request—a court ordered the Akron Art Institute to become the non-profit custodian of his work. This was the first time a museum had this responsibility for a living artist. An "ultra-modernist," as he preferred to classify himself, Sommer's art was a vital force in the developing May Show.

A Selection of Objects

2 Frank Nelson Wilcox.
The Old Market, 1920.
Sundry Purchase Fund. CMA 20.279

3 August F. Biehle.
Landscape–Cuyahoga River, 1921.
Mr. and Mrs. Frederick A. Biehle Collection.

4 August F. Biehle.
Egg Lady, 1922.
Mr. and Mrs. Frederick A.
Biehle Collection.

39 Henry George Keller.
Pigs in Orchard, ca. 1919.
Purchase, Dudley P. Allen Fund.
CMA 19.243

40 Frank Nelson Wilcox.
The Omnibus, ca. 1920.
Sundry Purchase Fund. CMA 20.281

Opposite

28/29 Alexander Blazys.
Russian Dancers, 1925.
Hinman B. Hurlbut Collection.
CMA 1547.26 & 1548.26

5 August F. Biehle.
The Flats, 1923.
Mr. and Mrs. Frederick A. Biehle Collection.

7 George Adomeit.
The Fishermen, 1924.
Lent by the Union Commerce Bank.

8 August F. Biehle.
Haystacks–Berlin Heights, 1924.
Boston, Mr. and Mrs. Jon Alder Collection.

9 Carl Frederick Gaertner.
The Furnace, 1924.
Lent by the Union Commerce Bank.

12 Carl Frederick Gaertner.
The Pie Wagon, 1926.
Gift of Mrs. Carl Gaertner. CMA 53.371

10 Henry George Keller.
The Madonna of Ivory, 1925.
Gift of Mrs. B. P. Ball. CMA 25.632

Paul B. Travis 1926

42 Paul Bough Travis.
Man's Head, 1926.
Gift of The Print Club. CMA 26.175

13 Frank Nelson Wilcox.
Washerwoman by the Loire, 1926.
Lent by the Union Commerce Bank.

14 William Eastman.
Eze, Cote d'Azur, 1927.
Lent by the Union Commerce Bank.

57 R. Guy Cowan.
Madonna and Child, 1928.
Cleveland, Mr. and Mrs. Lewis C. Williams Collection.

43 Jean Ulen.
Corfe Dorset, ca. 1930.
Gift of The Print Club. CMA 30.156

53 Henry George Keller.
Drawing No. 2, Study for painting:
"A Pastoral," ca. 1930.
Educational Purchase Fund. CMA 30.135

44 Stevan Dohanos.
Onions in Basket, ca. 1932.
Gift of The Print Club. CMA 32.150

45 Jean Ulen.
Wash Day, ca. 1932.
Gift of The Print Club. CMA 32.143

59 Viktor Schreckengost.
The Seasons: Vase, 1932.
Hinman B. Hurlbut Collection. CMA 964.32

15 Joseph B. Egan.
Sick Committee, 1933.
Purchase, The Cleveland Traveling
Exhibitions Fund. CMA 33.27

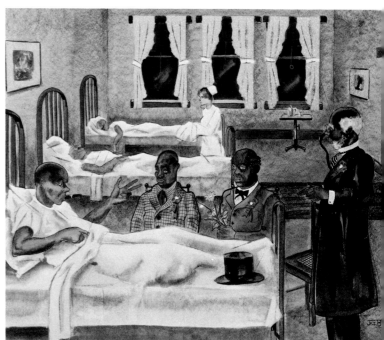

54

54 William Sommer.
Seated Man, 1936.
Hinman B. Hurlbut Collection. CMA 2027.47

17 William Sommer.
Calculation in Blue and Brown, ca. 1935-36.
Mr. and Mrs. Donald S. Boncela Collection.

61 Walter A. Sinz.
Beautiful Isle of Somewhere, 1940.
Purchase, Dudley P. Allen Fund. CMA 41.50

84 Edd A. Ruggles.
Steam and Smoke, ca. 1932.
Gift of Mrs. Edd A. Ruggles. CMA 72.1092

19 David Mink.
Landscape near Flats, 1940.
Purchase, The Cleveland Traveling
Exhibitions Fund. CMA 40.56

31 Viktor Schreckengost.
The Dictator, 1939.
Lent by the artist.

57

1941-1950

Right

55 William Sommer.
Pen Drawing of Nude, 1942.
Mr. and Mrs. Joseph Erdelac Collection.

Below

20 Paul B. Travis.
Congo Women, 1943.
Purchase, The Cleveland Traveling
Exhibitions Fund. CMA 43.221

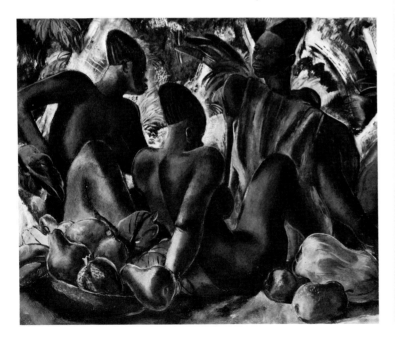

21 John Paul Miller.
Backward Glance, 1944.
Purchase, Silver Jubilee Treasure Fund. CMA 44.247

46 William E. Smith.
My Son, My Son, 1941.
Gift of The Print Club. CMA 41.122

33 Hugh Moore.
Mystic-Muse, 1949.
Gift of Mrs. B. P. Bole. CMA 49.62

63 Kenneth Francis Bates.
Hibiscus Bloom, 1944.
Bequest of Marie Odenkirk Clark. CMA 72.198

23 Peter Paul Dubaniewicz.
Still Life, 1947.
Purchase, The Cleveland Traveling Exhibitions Fund. CMA 47.85

64 Kenneth Francis Bates.
My Trip to Pittsburgh, undated.
Purchase, Dudley P. Allen Fund. CMA 45.45

66 Edris Eckhardt.
Introspection, ca. 1947.
Gift of Mrs. Paul Moore. CMA 47.103

65 Charles Bartley Jeffery.
Dish: Woodland Close-up, 1946.
Mary Spedding Milliken Memorial Collection,
Gift of William Mathewson Milliken. CMA 46.92

1951-1960

Right

70 John Paul Miller. *Necklace,* ca. 1953.
Silver Jubilee Treasure Fund;
Wishing Well Fund. CMA 53.181

Below

68 Doris Hall. *Marmorata,* 1951.
Mary Spedding Milliken Memorial Collection,
Gift of William Mathewson Milliken. CMA 51.133

69 Frederick A. Miller.
Candle Holder, ca. 1952.
Mary Spedding Milliken Memorial Collection,
Gift of William Mathewson Milliken. CMA 52.138

47 Roy Lichtenstein.
Hunter with Dog, 1952.
Mr. and Mrs. Henry Steinberg Collection.

64

65

Right
34 William M. McVey.
Rumination, 1957.
Purchase, Norman O. Stone and
Ella A. Stone Memorial Fund. CMA 57.185

Below
73 Frederick A. Miller.
Sugar Bowl with Cover and Creamer, 1957.
Silver Jubilee Treasure Fund; Wishing Well Fund.
CMA 57.170-.171

26 Victor Kord.
Composition No. 2, 1957.
Purchase, The Cleveland Traveling Exhibitions Fund.
CMA 58.253

48 Herbert Carroll Cassill.
Icarus, 1958.
Silver Jubilee Treasure Fund. CMA 58.248

1961-1975

78 Toshiko Takaezu.
Plate No. 7, 1961.
Gift of the Ohio Northern Chapter,
American Institute of Interior Designers.
CMA 61.98

77 Claude Conover.
Terrace Bottle, 1961.
Gift of the Cleveland
Art Association.
CMA 62.71

27 Richard Lazzaro.
Pig Lady, 1962.
Purchase, Wishing Well Fund. CMA 62.65

56 Edwin Mieczkowski.
Palestime, 1963.
The Harold T. Clark Educational
Extension Fund. CMA 64.139

69

79 Howard William Kottler. *Bottle,* 1963.
Gift of the Ohio Northern Chapter,
American Institute of Interior Designers. CMA 63.269

50 Jean Kubota Cassill.
Barren Landscape, ca. 1964.
Wishing Well Fund. CMA 64.126

71

Right
38 David Davis.
Harmonic Grid XXV, 1974.
Mr. and Mrs. Joseph Erdelac Collection.

Below
87 Nicholas C. Hlobeczy.
Plum Tree, 1965.
Sundry Purchase Fund. CMA 66.217

85 Irving Achorn.
Michael Murphy, 1965.
Gift of Jacob Wattenmaker. CMA 66.216

81 Charles Lakofsky.
Covered Jar, 1967.
Gift of the Cleveland Art Association.
CMA 67.196,a

82 Howard William Kottler.
Homage to Gertrude, 1973.
Cleveland, Mrs. Jacob Friedman Collection.

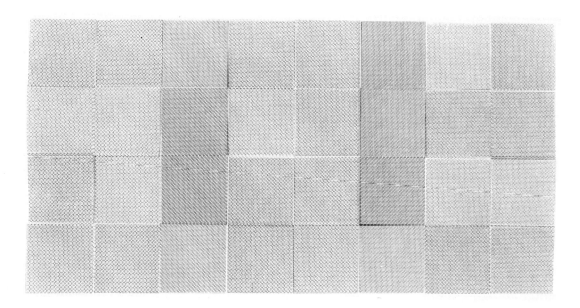

51 John Pearson.
Screen Series No. 6, 1971.
Mr. and Mrs. Henry Steinberg Collection.

83 Janet E. Trisler.
Milk Carton, 1973.
Cleveland, Dr. Edward A. Hinkle Collection.

Waiting for the opening
of the Patrons' Preview
for the 43rd May Show, 1961.
Photo: Frank Reed.

Catalog

Listing is chronological by date of the execution of an art work within the categories. An asterisk (*) indicates that the object is illustrated.

PAINTING

1 Charles Shackleton, 1856-1920. *Over the Dunes.* Oil, 1919, 28-1/2 x 30-1/2 inches (72.4 x 77.4 cm.). Gift from the Cleveland Art Association. 19.240

2 Frank Nelson Wilcox, 1887-1964. *The Old Market.* Oil, 1920, 28-3/4 x 22-3/4 inches (73 x 57.8 cm.). Sundry Purchase Fund. 20.279*

3 August F. Biehle, 1895- . *Landscape–Cuyahoga River.* Oil, 1921, 22 x 28 inches (55.9 x 71.1 cm.). Mr. and Mrs. Frederick A. Biehle Collection.*

4 August F. Biehle, 1895- . *Egg Lady.* Oil, 1922, 17 x 14 inches (43.2 x 35.5 cm.). Mr. and Mrs. Frederick A. Biehle Collection.*

5 August F. Biehle, 1895- . *The Flats.* Oil, 1923, 14 x 15 inches (35.5 x 38.1 cm.). Mr. and Mrs. Frederick A. Biehle Collection.*

6 Henry George Keller, 1869-1949. *Still Life (October).* Oil, 1923, 24 x 28-1/2 inches (61 x 72.4 cm.). Mr. and Mrs. Joseph Erdelac Collection.

7 George Adomeit, n.d. *The Fishermen.* Oil on canvas, 1924, 29-1/2 x 33-1/2 inches (74.9 x 85.1 cm.). Lent by the Union Commerce Bank.*

8 August F. Biehle, 1895- . *Haystacks–Berlin Heights.* Oil, 1924, 28-1/2 x 39-1/2 inches (72.4 x 100.3 cm.). Boston, Mr. and Mrs. Jon Alder Collection.*

9 Carl Frederick Gaertner, 1898-1952. *The Furnace.* Oil on canvas, 1924, 34-1/2 x 40-1/2 inches (87.6 x 102.8 cm.). Lent by the Union Commerce Bank.*

10 Henry George Keller, 1869-1949. *The Madonna of Ivory.* Oil, 1925, 30-1/2 x 25 inches (77.5 x 63.5 cm.). Gift of Mrs. B. P. Ball. 25.632*

11 Sandor Vago, n.d. *Chinese Girl.* Oil on canvas, 1925, 39-1/2 x 33-1/2 inches (100.3 x 85.1 cm.). Lent by the Union Commerce Bank.

12 Carl Frederick Gaertner, 1898-1952. *The Pie Wagon.* Oil, 1926, 41-5/8 x 60-1/4 inches (105.7 x 153 cm.). Gift of Mrs. Carl Gaertner. 53.371*

13 Frank Nelson Wilcox, 1887-1964. *Washerwoman by the Loire.* Oil on canvas, 1926, 28 x 35-1/2 inches (71.1 x 90. 2 cm.). Lent by the Union Commerce Bank.*

14 William Eastman, n.d. *Eze, Cote d'Azur.* Oil on canvas, 1927, 32-1/2 x 35-3/4 inches (82.5 x 90.8 cm.). Lent by the Union Commerce Bank.*

15 Joseph B. Egan, 1906- . *Sick Committee.* Water color, 1933, 20 x 25-1/2 inches (50.8 x 64.8 cm.). Purchase, The Cleveland Traveling Exhibitions Fund. 33.27*

16 Henry George Keller, 1869-1949. *Storm Frightened Animals.* Oil, 1933, 30-1/16 x 40 inches (76.3 x 101.6 cm.). Purchase from the J. H. Wade Fund. 34.56

17 William Sommer, 1867-1949. *Calculation in Blue and Brown.* Water color, ca. 1935-36, 12-1/2 x 19 inches (31.7 x 48.2 cm.). Mr. and Mrs. Donald S. Boncela Collection.*

18 Morton G. Winslow, 1899-   . *Built in 1816*. Water color, 1937, 30 x 37-7/8 inches (76.2 x 96.2 cm.). Purchase, The Cleveland Traveling Exhibitions Fund. 37.8

19 David Mink, 1912-   . *Landscape near Flats*. Water color, 1940, 29-1/4 x 37-1/2 inches (74.3 x 95.7 cm.). Purchase, The Cleveland Traveling Exhibitions Fund. 40.56*

20 Paul B. Travis, 1891-   . *Congo Women*. Oil, 1943, 30-1/2 x 39-1/2 inches (77.5 x 100.3 cm.). Purchase, The Cleveland Traveling Exhibitions Fund. 43.221*

21 John Paul Miller, 1918-   . *Backward Glance*. Water color, 1944, 19-3/4 x 4-1/2 inches (50.2 x 11.4 cm.). Purchase, Silver Jubilee Treasure Fund. 44.247*

22 Edward Dobrotka, 1918-   . *Rougham Timberyard, Gulfport, Mississippi*. Water color, 1945, 10-1/4 x 15 inches (26 x 38.1 cm.). Purchase, Silver Jubilee Treasure Fund. 45.51

23 Peter Paul Dubaniewiez, 1913-   . *Still Life*. Encaustic, 1947, 16 x 36 inches (40.6 x 91.4 cm.). Purchase, The Cleveland Traveling Exhibitions Fund. 47.85*

24 Glen Moore Shaw, 1891-   . *Sic Transit Gloria Mundi*. Water color, 1952, 21-1/2 x 26 inches (54.6 x 66 cm.). Purchase, Silver Jubilee Treasure Fund. 52.130

25 Shirley Aley Campbell, 1925-   . *Requiem for Dominic*. Water color, tempera, and pen on masonite, 1957, 40 x 26 inches (101.6 x 66 cm.). Purchase, The Silver Jubilee Treasure Fund. 57.174*

26 Victor Kord, 1935-   . *Composition No. 2*. Water color, 1957, 20-1/2 x 13-1/8 inches (52 x 33.3 cm.). Purchase, The Cleveland Traveling Exhibitions Fund. 58.253*

27 Richard Lazzaro, 1937-   . *Pig Lady*. Oil, 1962, 47 x 35-3/16 inches (119.4 x 89.4 cm.). Purchase, Wishing Well Fund. 62.65*

SCULPTURE

28 Alexander Blazys, 1894-1963. *Russian Dancer*. Bronze, 1925, H. 12-1/4 inches (31.1 cm.). Hinman B. Hurlbut Collection. 1548.26*

29 Alexander Blazys, 1894-1963. *Russian Dancer*. Bronze, 1925, W. 11-1/2 inches (29.2 cm.). Hinman B. Hurlbut Collection. 1547.26*

30 Alexander Blazys, 1894-1963. *Legia*. Bronze, 1928, L. 17 inches (43.2 cm.). Lent by the Union Commerce Bank.

31 Viktor Schreckengost, 1906-   . *The Dictator*. Direct ceramic modeling in red clay with raw borax glaze and engobe, 1939, D. 14 inches (35.5 cm.). Lent by the artist.*

32 Sol A. Bauer, 1898-   . *Seated Figure*. Wood, ca. 1942, H. 13 inches (33 cm.). Purchase, Dudley P. Allen Fund. 42.202

33 Hugh Moore, 1916-   . *Mystic-Muse*. Plaster, 1949, H. 9-1/4 inches (23.5 cm.). Gift of Mrs. B. P. Bole. 49.62*

34 William M. McVey, 1905-   . *Rumination*. White marble, 1957, H. 32 inches (81.3 cm.). Purchase, Norman O. Stone and Ella A. Stone Memorial Fund. 57.185*

35 John Clague, 1928-   . *Progression in Black and White*. Painted steel, 1963, H. 68 inches (172.7 cm.). Wishing Well Fund. 63.267*

36 George Brewster, 1940-   . *Torso*. Wood and metal, 1965, H. 52 inches (132.1 cm.). Gift of the Cleveland Art Association. 66.212

37 Jerome Aidlin, 1935-   . *Wine Flowers*. Bronze, ca. 1966, H. 24 inches (61 cm.). Wishing Well Fund. 66.209

38 David Davis, 1920-   . *Harmonic Grid XXV*. Corten steel, 1974, H. 96 inches (244 cm.). Mr. and Mrs. Joseph Erdelac Collection.*

PRINTS

39 Henry George Keller, 1869-1949. *Pigs in Orchard.* Etching, ca. 1919, 4-1/4 x 5-1/4 inches (10.8 x 13.3 cm.). Purchase, Dudley P. Allen Fund. 19.243*

40 Frank N. Wilcox, 1887-1964. *The Omnibus.* Etching, ca. 1920, 7 x 8-5/16 inches (17.8 x 22.6 cm.). Sundry Purchase Fund. 20.281*

41 Orville Houghton Peets, 1884-1968. *The River Wall, Oporto.* Etching, ca. 1926, 9-7/16 x 7-1/16 inches (24.0 x 18.0 cm.). Gift of The Print Club. 26.172

42 Paul Bough Travis, 1891-1975. *Man's Head.* Lithograph, 1926, 12 x 13-1/2 inches (30.5 x 34.3 cm.). Gift of The Print Club. 26.175*

43 Jean Ulen, 1900- . *Corfe Dorset.* Etching and aquatint, ca. 1930, 9 x 10-11/16 inches (22.9 x 27.1 cm.). Gift of The Print Club. 30.156*

44 Stevan Dohanos, 1907- . *Onions in Basket.* Linoleum cut, ca. 1932, 4-13/16 x 6-5/8 inches (12.2 x 16.8 cm.). Gift of The Print Club. 32.150*

45 Jean Ulen, 1900- . *Wash Day.* Etching and aquatint, ca. 1932, 8-3/8 x 11 inches (21.2 x 28 cm.). Gift of The Print Club. 32.143*

46 William E. Smith, 1913- . *My Son, My Son.* Linoleum cut, 1941, 7-13/16 x 5-7/16 inches (19.8 x 13.8 cm.). Gift of The Print Club. 41.122*

47 Roy Lichtenstein, 1923- . *Hunter with Dog.* Color woodcut, 1952, 15-1/2 x 17 inches (39.3 x 43.2 cm.). Mr. and Mrs. Henry Steinberg Collection.*

48 Herbert Carroll Cassill, 1928- . *Icarus.* Mixed media intaglio, 1958, 27-7/8 x 21 inches (70.8 x 53.3 cm.). Silver Jubilee Treasure Fund. 58.248*

49 Herbert Carroll Cassill, 1928- . *To a New World.* Mixed media intaglio, ca. 1960, 23-13/16 x 17-7/8 inches (60.6 x 45.3 cm.). Gift of the Cleveland Art Association. 60.65

50 Jean Kubota Cassill, 1926- . *Barren Landscape.* Mixed media intaglio, ca. 1964, 23-7/8 x 21-1/4 inches (60.7 x 54 cm.). Wishing Well Fund. 64.126*

51 John Pearson, 1940- . *Screen Series No. 6.* Silk screen, 1971, 14-1/2 x 27-1/4 inches (36.8 x 69.2 cm.). Mr. and Mrs. Henry Steinberg Collection.*

52 Gary Sawyer, n.d. *Melisande.* Embossed print, 17 x 11-1/2 inches (43.2 x 29.2 cm.). Mrs. Bernice Kent Collection.

53 Henry George Keller, 1869-1949. *Drawing No. 2, Study for Painting: "A Pastoral."* Drawing, ca. 1930, 29-1/2 x 40 inches (74.9 x 101.6 cm.). Educational Purchase Fund. 30.135*

54 William Sommer, 1867-1949. *Seated Man.* Pen and ink drawing, 1936, 21 x 12-15/16 inches (53.3 x 32.9 cm.). Hinman B. Hurlbut Collection. 2027.47*

55 William Sommer, 1867-1949. *Pen Drawing of Nude.* Pen and ink, 1942, 20 x 11-1/4 inches (50.8 x 28.6 cm.). Mr. and Mrs. Joseph Erdelac Collection.*

56 Edwin Mieczkowski, 1929- . *Palestime.* Ink drawing, 1963, 17-1/2 x 24 inches (44.5 x 61 cm.). The Harold T. Clark Educational Extension Fund. 64.139*

DECORATIVE ARTS

57 R. Guy Cowan, 1884- . *Madonna and Child.* Ceramic, 1928, H. 19 inches (48.3 cm.). Cleveland, Mr. and Mrs. Lewis C. Williams Collection.*

58 Cowan Pottery. *Vase* (one of a pair). Faience, 1930, H. 11 inches (28 cm.). Mr. and Mrs. Joseph Erdelac Collection.

59 Viktor Schreckengost, 1906- . *The Seasons: Vase.* Stoneware, 1932, H. 11-5/8 inches (29.5 cm.). Hinman B. Hurlbut Collection. 964.32*

60 Edward H. Winter, 1908- . *Transparent Emerald Green Bowl.* Enamel, 1936, 6-1/2 x 16-1/2 inches (16.5 x 41.9 cm.). Mary Spedding Milliken Collection, Gift of William Mathewson Milliken. 36.373

61 Walter A. Sinz, 1881- . *Beautiful Isle of Somewhere.* Ceramic, 1940, H. 13-1/2 inches (34.3 cm.). Purchase, Dudley P. Allen Fund. 41.50*

62 Edward H. Winter, 1908- . *Pomegranate.* Transparent and opaque enamel and copper, 1940, D. 9-3/4 inches (24.7 cm.). Bequest of Marie Odenkirk Clark. 72.1208

63 Kenneth Francis Bates, 1904- . *Hibiscus Bloom.* Enamel, 1944, D. 11 inches (28 cm.). Bequest of Marie Odenkirk Clark. 72.198*

64 Kenneth Francis Bates, 1904- . *My Trip to Pittsburgh.* Plaque, enamel on silver, ca. 1945, 5 x 5 inches (12.7 x 12.7 cm.). Purchase, Dudley P. Allen Fund. 45.45*

65 Charles Bartley Jeffery, 1910- . *Dish: Woodland Close-up.* Enamel, 1946, D. 5-7/8 inches (14.9 cm.). Mary Spedding Milliken Memorial Collection, Gift of William Mathewson Milliken. 46.92*

66 Edris Eckhardt, 1907- . *Introspection.* Ceramic, ca. 1947, H. 16-3/8 inches (41.6 cm.). Gift of Mrs. Paul Moore. 47.103*

67 Charles Bartley Jeffery, 1910- . *Wall Cross: Deposition and Angels.* Silver gilt, copper, transparent and opaque enamels, and paillon, 1948, W. 4-3/8 inches (11.1 cm.). Bequest of Marie Odenkirk Clark. 72.1200

68 Doris Hall, 1907- . *Marmorata.* Enamel, 1951, D. 7-3/16 inches (18.3 cm.). Mary Spedding Milliken Memorial Collection, Gift of William Mathewson Milliken. 51.133*

69 Frederick A. Miller, 1913- . *Candle Holder.* Silver, ca. 1952, D. 3-15/16 inches (10 cm.). Mary Spedding Milliken Memorial Collection, Gift of William Mathewson Milliken. 52.138*

70 John Paul Miller, 1918- . *Necklace.* Gold, ca. 1953, 17 inches, pendant 2-3/4 x 1-3/4 inches (43.2, 7 x 4.4 cm.). Silver Jubilee Treasure Fund; Wishing Well Fund. 53.181*

71 Viktor Schreckengost, 1906- . *Lake: Jar.* Stoneware, 1955, H. 9-3/4 inches (24.7 cm.). The Mary Spedding Milliken Memorial Collection, Gift of William Mathewson Milliken. 55.224

72 Kenneth Francis Bates, 1904- . *Masquerade.* Bronze, copper, fine gold, opaque and transparent enamels, and paillon, 1956, H. 4 inches (10.2 cm.). Bequest of Marie Odenkirk Clark. 72.1188,a

73 Frederick A. Miller, 1913- . *Sugar Bowl with Cover.* Sterling silver, 1957, 2-15/16 x 2-3/8 inches (7.5 x 6 cm.). Silver Jubilee Treasure Fund; Wishing Well Fund. 57.170*

74 Frederick A. Miller, 1913- . *Creamer.* Sterling silver, 1957, 3-1/2 x 2 inches (8.9 x 5.1 cm.). Silver Jubilee Treasure Fund; Wishing Well Fund. 57.171*

75 Jean O'Hara, n.d. *Vase.* Enamel, 1959, H. 7 inches (17.8 cm.). Gift of the Cleveland Art Association. 59.160*

76 Jean O'Hara, n.d. *Etched Copper No. 3.* Enamel, ca. 1959, H. 7 inches (17.8 cm.). Bequest of Marie Odenkirk Clark. TR 15772/63*

77 Claude Conover, 1907- . *Terrace Bottle.* Stoneware, 1961, H. 15-3/4 inches (40 cm.). Gift of the Cleveland Art Association. 62.71*

78 Toshiko Takaezu, 1922- . *Plate No. 7.* Stoneware, 1961, D. 13-3/4 inches (34.9 cm.). Gift of the Ohio Northern Chapter, American Institute of Interior Designers. 61.98*

79 Howard William Kottler, 1930- . *Bottle.* Stoneware, 1963, D. 25-1/4 inches (64.1 cm.). Gift of the Ohio Northern Chapter, American Institute of Interior Designers. 63.269*

80 Charles Lakofsky, 1922- . *Covered Jar.* Porcelain, 1966, H. 7-3/4 inches (19.7 cm.). Mary Spedding Milliken Memorial Collection, Gift of William Mathewson Milliken. 66.211*

81 Charles Lakofsky, 1922-   . *Covered Jar.* Porcelain, 1967, H. 7-3/8 inches (18.7 cm.). Gift of The Cleveland Art Association. 67.196,a*

82 Howard William Kottler, 1930-   . *Homage to Gertrude.* Porcelain, ceramic decals, silver lustre, leather, and plastic, 1973, D. 10-1/4 inches (26 cm.). Cleveland, Mrs. Jacob Friedman Collection.*

83 Janet E. Trisler, n.d. *Milk Carton.* Stoneware, 1973, H. 10 inches (25.4 cm.). Cleveland, Dr. Edward A. Hinkle Collection.*

84 Edd A. Ruggles, 1880-1940. *Steam and Smoke.* Photograph, silver print, and soft focus lens, ca. 1932, 10-1/8 x 12-11/16 inches (25.7 x 32.2 cm.). Gift of Mrs. Edd A. Ruggles. 72.1092*

85 Irving Achorn, 1920-   . *Michael Murphy.* Photograph, 1965, 8-1/2 x 7 inches (21.6 x 17.8 cm.). Gift of Jacob Wattenmaker. 66.216*

86 Tony Buck, 1925-   . *Fantasy No. 4.* Photograph, ca. 1965, 11 x 14 inches (28 x 35.5 cm.). Wishing Well Fund. 65.42

87 Nicholas C. Hlobeczy, 1927-   . *Plum Tree.* Photograph, 1965, 7-5/16 x 9-3/8 inches (18.6 x 23.8 cm.). Sundry Purchase Fund. 66.217*

88 Frank Tichy, 1924-   . *Aspens.* Photograph, 1965, 9-1/2 x 7 inches (24.1 x 17.8 cm.). Wishing Well Fund. 65.41

89 Bertram S. Koslen, n.d. *Antikt Kuriosa.* Photograph, 1970, 28 x 31-1/2 inches (71.1 x 80 cm.). Mr. and Mrs. Joseph Erdelac Collection.

TEXTILES

90 Dorothy Turobinski, n.d. *Golden Shadows.* Wool and silk, ca. 1959, 38 x 113 inches (96.5 x 286.9 cm.). Silver Jubilee Treasure Fund; Wishing Well Fund. 59.144

91 Dorothy Turobinski, n.d. *How Many Colors Are One Plus Three?* Wool, ca. 1965, 40 x 118 inches (101.6 x 299.7 cm.). Gift of the Cleveland Art Association. 65.71

Publications of the Art History and Education Department

American Japonism: Contacts Between America and Japan 1854-1910 by Carol Clark. 16 pp., 7 x 8 inches, 10 illus., 1975.

Arms and Armor in The Cleveland Museum of Art by Martin Linsey and Norma J. Roberts. 20 pp., 7-1/2 x 9 inches, 49 illus., 1974.

Aspects of 19th-Century Sculpture by H. W. Janson with the assistance of Christine Bishop, Holly Strawbridge, Kenneth Pearson, Laurel Diznoff, Pamela Barboutis, and Tom L. Johnson. 32pp., 7-1/2 x 9 inches, 28 illus., 1975.

Between Past and Present: French, English, and American Etching 1850-1950 by Gabriel P. Weisberg and Ronnie L. Zakon. 74 pp., 7-1/4 x 8-1/2 inches, 50 illus., 1977. LC 76-53113, ISBN 910386-33-1.

In the Nature of Materials: Japanese Decorative Arts by Marjorie Williams. 41 pp., 8-3/4 x 11 inches, 32 illus., 1977.

An Introduction to American Art in The Cleveland Museum of Art by Celeste Adams, Rita Myers, and Adele Z. Silver. 20 pp., 7-1/2 x 9 inches, 36 illus., 1972.

An Introduction to The Art of Indian Asia in The Cleveland Museum of Art by Adele Z. Silver. 16 pp., 7-1/2 x 9 inches, 19 illus., undated.

An Introduction to The Arts of Africa and Oceania by Emelia Sica and Evelyn Mitchell. 16 pp., 7-1/2 x 9 inches, 23 illus., 1973.

Materials and Techniques of 20th-Century Artists by Dee Driscole, Dorothy Ross, under the Guidance of Gabriel P. Weisberg, Andrew T. Chakalis, Karen Smith, and June Hargrove. 48 pp., 7-1/2 x 9 inches, 31 illus., 1976.

Traditions and Revisions: Themes from the History of Sculpture by Gabriel P. Weisberg, with an Introduction by H. W. Janson. 144 pp., 8-1/4 x 10-1/2 inches, 119 illus. (2 color), 1975. LC 75-26708, ISBN 0-910386-23-4.

For information on ordering any of these titles or other books about the Museum, please contact the Museum Sales Desk, The Cleveland Museum of Art, 11150 East Boulevard, Cleveland, Ohio 44106.